Page 2: A young Brahmin contemplates the life of the spirit at the Chidambaram Temple.
Pages 4-5: Thousands say their prayers to Brahma the Creator at the sacred lake
in Pushkar.
Page 6: A veiled woman outside her mud and thatch house in Rajasthan.
Pages 8-9: Bibi ka Maqbara, the mausoleum that Emperor Aurangzeb built for his wife,
was intended to replicate the grandeur of the Taj.

PHOTO CREDITS

All photographs in this book are from **Fredrik Arvidsson** except for the following: pages 13, 14, 15 (top), 24-25, 27 (centre), 35, 39, 40-41, 45, 47 (bottom), 51 (bottom left), 55 (right, top and bottom), 56 (main picture), 59 (top left), 60-61, 67 (bottom), 71 (bottom and centre right), 74 (bottom), 75 (bottom right), 77 (bottom left), 83 (top right and bottom), 84 (top), 88 (bottom), 97 (top left), 100 (top left and centre), 105 (bottom right), 107 (top left and right), 112 (bottom right), 113 (bottom), 114 (bottom), 116 (top right and centre), 117, 119 (inset), 129 (top and centre), 122 (bottom), 123 (second from top, bottom), 124, 125 (bottom left and right), 127 (centre and bottom left), 129, 130, 131, 132, 133, 134, 135, 136, 137, 139, 140, 141, **Photobank, Luca Invernizzi Tettoni**; 46: B.N. Khazanchi; 47 (top and centre), 51 (top), 57 (top left and centre left): E. Hanumantha Rao; 48-49 (main picture); 49 (inset), 50 (top right), 53 (top, bottom left and right), 54 (bottom), 57 (centre right and bottom): Joanna Van Gruisen; 51 (centre, top right): Ajay Khullar; 52 (bottom): R.S. Chandawak; 53 (centre, top right), 57 (top right), 59 (top right): C.R. Anantha Padmanabha Rao; 57 (centre, middle): Rajeev Ohri; 58 (top right): Ashok Nath; 58 (bottom): Aditya Arya; 59 (centre): Marie Sonza; 59 (bottom): S. G. Neginhal; 87 (top): Akhil Bakshi—all the preceding from **Fotomedia**; 34 (top right), 38 (bottom left), 52 (top right), 53 (centre, top right), 63, 64 (bottom), 65 (third row, 2nd & 3rd pictures), 80 (top), 88 (centre), 92 (top left and right, bottom left), 108 (bottom), 125 (top), 127 (top), **Peter G. Needham**; 28 (top left), 64 (top right), 65 (third row, 1st picture, fourth row, 2nd picture), 66 (top), 71 (top left and centre left), 78 (top right), 83 (top left and bottom right), 86 (except top), 92 (centre left), 120 (bottom), **Dinesh Khanna**; 25 (inset), 29, 38 (bottom right), **Life File**; 71 (top right), 95 (bottom), **HBL Network**; 30, 32 (bottom right), **Art Directors**; 84 (centre), 92 (bottom right), **Richard I'Anson**; 50 (top right) Joginder Chawla; 51 (bottom right): **Veronique Sanson**; 81 (top) **Camera Press**; 87 (bottom) **Hutchison Library**; 12, **Hulton Deutsch**; 113 (top right), **Susanna Burton**; 97 (bottom), **G.C. Nanda & Sons Pte Ltd**

INDIA: PLAYGROUND OF THE GODS

© 1996 Times Editions Pte Ltd

Published by Times Editions
an imprint of Times Editions Pte Ltd
Times Centre, 1 New Industrial Road
Singapore 536196

Series Editor: K E Tan
Designer: Tuck Loong
Production Manager: Anthoney Chua
Colour separation by Eray Scan Pte Ltd, Singapore
Printed in Singapore

ISBN: 981 204 735 2

INDIA

PLAYGROUND OF THE GODS

INDIA
PLAYGROUND OF THE GODS

Text
RAHUL PATHAK

Photographs
FREDRIK ARVIDSSON
PHOTOBANK
LUCA INVERNIZZI TETTONI

and

FOTOMEDIA, PETER G. NEEDHAM, DINESH KHANNA

TIMES EDITIONS

CONTENTS

INTRODUCTION

No land has been conquered more often or more completely than India. For 4,000 years, its armies have been routed by almost every single invader who has thundered down its plains. But here lies the twist. While those victors have vanished and other contemporary civilisations have ceased to exist, India, the perennial loser, has survived and actually gained muscle from its defeats. This seeming contradiction is the key to understanding the country.

Something about this land converted its conquerors. Practically every invader ended up as an Indian. Those who came as marauders ended up as defenders. And that has been India's greatest strength. It has accepted and absorbed foreign influences until they became an integral part of her.

This live and let live attitude explains why the country has survived so long. But it also tells you something about its character. For example, it explains the endless patience and the incredible resilience of the people and their conviction that some good must come out of everything. It tells you something of this contrary land that wallows in defeat, turns personal tragedy into something as sublime as the Taj Mahal and has conjured up a vibrant religion based on suffering. The land whose history has been written in blood has also produced the Buddha.

These invasions also served to make India one of the most diverse countries in the world. The settlers who came from all parts of the world did not abandon their individuality. So not only does one see different faces and different races, one also gets to see dazzlingly different customs and traditions which have lingered from their half-forgotten past. It is no accident that the land that produced the *Kamasutra* also put its women behind the veil. Quite simply, the conservatives and the iconoclasts have both had their day in India, where there has always been room for different schools of thought.

Pointing to this, India's first prime minister Jawaharlal Nehru wrote: "The diversity of India is tremendous. It is obvious. It lies on the surface and anyone can see it." He spoke not just of the people and their ways, but also of the land that echoes these fluctuating mood swings.

A short flight can take you from shimmering mountains, across a stark desert to choppy seas. A dart of the eye can transport you from the grubby hovels of the poor to the tremulous beauty of ancient monuments. And even while you are gazing tenderly at the graceful deer of the Sunderbans, the sudden roar of the Bengal Tiger might strike a chill in your bones.

Bemused by such diversity and contrast, some outsiders tend to label India a land of wonder and mystery. But really, the only mystery is how, in spite of so many differences, 900 million people with their 330 million deities have managed to develop and assert something common, an "Indianness". And the wonder is that it has lasted so long, gathering verve and colour, creating art and beauty along the way.

The bustle of life can leave you breathless. Left: Sarees hitched above their knees, fishwives from Goa hurry through another busy day. Above: Exhausted by the day's labours, a businessman grabs some rest in New Delhi's Connaught Place.

HISTORY AND THE INDIANS

Indians are obsessed with their history. They don't see it as a drab litany of dates and facts expounded in classrooms. Rather, to them history is the stuff of wars and heroes, of men and gods and of romantic legends that have been passed on from father to son. The legends burst forth in ballads and village plays, get dramatised on television and perpetuated at religious gatherings until, in the end, many people believe them.

Thus, an Indian will tell you with complete conviction that 125,000 years ago a great battle was fought between the forces of good and evil in the agrarian town of Kurukshetra—and good triumphed. He will describe the weapons used, the strategies employed and the many many deceits that decided the war. Or he will point to the exact spot in Ayodhya where Lord Rama was supposed to have been born aeons ago, identify the kitchen where his food was cooked and show you the very cave in which he rested. In the same breath, he will narrate the historically recorded invasion by Alexander the Great or the coming of the first Mughals.

Myth, legend, history and religion mean one and the same thing to him. All of them have been kept alive by a robust storytelling tradition until folk history has become wonderfully complex and colourful.

Archaeologists and historians will point out that while India's history might not be quite as ancient as Indians would like to believe ("when Gods walked the earth"), it is certainly among the oldest in the world.

There is evidence that around 4,000 B.C., men in the northwest corner of India made the great leap from nomadic hunting to agriculture. They pottered about in this primitive village culture for about a thousand years, all the while sowing the seeds of something far more dramatic. Then, all of a sudden, these seeds blossomed into the mighty Indus Valley Civilisation, a civilisation which was among the most ancient and advanced in the world.

This civilisation, along the River Indus, was much larger in size and scope than its counterpart in Egypt. It had magnificent seaports, with docks almost 300 metres long and controlling sluice gates that ensured you could load ships at high tide or low. It had timber and lapis lazuli to trade. Its soapstone seals, with exquisite pictographs, have turned up in Iran and Mesopotamia. And it had two sprawling predecessors to the metropolises of the world—Harappa and Mohenjodaro.

Both cities, with populations touching 20,000, were proud of their artists and architects. Each had a citadel, as high as a five-storey building. They had indoor toilets, underground drains and brick houses decorated with beautiful bronze figurines and terracotta toys. No civilisation had even touched such sophistication.

But it died as suddenly as it had come up, choked in its prime by India's first invaders—the Aryans. Around 1500 B.C., the Aryans, the tall, fair-skinned nomads from central Asia, thundered down the plains on their horses and smashed the citadels that guarded the cities of Indus. The horse, which

History keeps turning full circles in India. Above: Native armies were overpowered by the British, as in the battle of Seringaptnam in 1799. Left: In 1947, Gandhi's freedom movement reclaimed the land for Indians.

the Harappans had never seen, and the iron axes of the invaders proved too powerful for the peace-loving settlers of Indus. Historians say they moved further south while the Aryans, like most future invaders of India, simply settled down and stayed put.

The Aryans were simple herdsmen when they first came, with none of the elegance or sophistication of the culture they had uprooted. But over the next one thousand years, they settled down to compile a vast body of beliefs, a huge pantheon of gods, an immense storehouse of ritual, four tomes known as the Vedas and the religion now known as Hinduism.

Just when Hinduism had formalised itself, with its hierarchy of priests and outcastes, Gautama Buddha, "the Enlightened One", was born in the foothills of the Himalayas in the sixth century B.C. He offered a drastically different alternative—a religion without caste, without violence, without worship and without a god. Of course, after his death his followers deified him. Even so the Buddha had a stunning impact on Hinduism, which then started to preach against violence.

The sixth century B.C. brought in other changes as well. The Persians rode in through the Hindu Kush mountains and conquered Punjab and the Indus Valley. They ruled for more than 200 years, before they were overthrown by the Greek forces of Alexander the Great. It was only after Alexander's death that Indian rule returned to India.

The reign of Ashoka, Emperor of Peace, of the Mauryan dynasty was around the corner and Buddhism was about to see the world. It was Ashoka who first made Buddhism a missionary faith, sending his emissaries to Egypt and Greece. He succeeded in converting the king of Ceylon and it was from there that the religion spread to the rest of the world. But Ashoka's true greatness lies in the fact that despite being such a committed Buddhist, he continued to respect other religions. He wrote: "All sects deserve reverence for one reason or another. By thus acting, a man exalts his own sect and at the same time does service to the sects of other people". These sentiments, and his revulsion at violence still endures as a powerful memory and one of Ashoka's monuments—four fierce lions—is now India's official seal.

The British and the French battled for control over India through much of the 18th century. Above: As this vintage map shows, the French had vast pockets of influence in India. They propped up their nominees as part of a shadow war against Britain.

14

Though the empire dissolved after Ashoka's death, some of his descendants, the Guptas, revived it many years later. Their reign over a vast chunk of present-day India between A.D. 320 and 467 has been called India's Golden Age. Never before, or since, has there been a period of greater peace or prosperity in India, or an outburst of literature so spectacular or the sparkle of art more intense. During this age, says one historian, India was possibly "the happiest and most civilised region in the world". And, perhaps, too rich for its own good. It was ripe for pillaging.

The first onslaught came from the "White Huns" of Central Asia, who overthrew the Gupta dynasty. They tore down temples, ripped apart palaces, smashed delicate sculptures and ransacked the treasury. But more importantly, they left India without a strong empire to defend itself against future invaders. The vacuum left by the Guptas was filled by a handful of bickering clans, who would be powerless against any strong adversary.

Meanwhile, the armies of Islam were gathering. From the eighth century onward, the Arabians and the Turks came in waves and met no resistance. At first, these were just merciless plundering forays. But in the 12th century Mohammed Ghori defeated all the Hindu armies who stood in his path —and then decided to stay put.

India had been invaded before and invariably the conquerors, whether Bactrians, Scythians or Huns, had accepted Hinduism and carved out their own niche in the caste hierarchy. But Mohammed Ghori and the Muslim rulers who followed him were different. On the question of religion, they would not budge. They stuck by Islam, even converting some Hindus to their fold. Every one of them resisted the spell of Hinduism. This had never happened before in India.

Different Muslim dynasties were to rule India until the 19th century. The most prominent of these were the mighty Mughals, whose rule spanned 300 years. During this period, a unique synthesis of cultures took place. While Islam spread, Hinduism did not retreat. And the greatest of Mughal rulers, Akbar, made friends with Hindu princes even as he ruled over them. He allowed both religions to flourish, preparing the ground for India as we know it today.

In fact, it was only during the Mughal rule that southern India was first touched by the happenings in the north. Before this, apart from being enveloped by Hinduism, it had always remained a world apart. Throughout history no one had managed to breach the area beyond the Deccan Plateau which was ruled by three independent kingdoms, the Cholas, the Pandyas and the Cheras. The people came from a different ethnic stock, spoke a different family of languages. It was Shah Jahan, the Mughal better known for giving the world the Taj Mahal, who first annexed large areas of the south.

Still, it was only after the all-conquering British armies came that the map of India first resembled its present shape. Till then the Mughals had ruled over about half of contemporary India, while the rest was carved up between scores of battling principalities. The British came in as traders of silks and spices, went on to become protectors of some squabbling nabobs and soon ended up as rulers of the vast and once unmanageable land as kingdom after kingdom surrendered to them.

For the first time in its history, India was ruled by a single entity. On the flip side, for the first time it had rulers who had no intention of making it their home. Indians look upon this 200-year period with mixed feelings. Some say it impoverished the land, as local industry was stifled, unable to compete with the sophisticated British industry. Others say that for the first time institutions such as the police, the judiciary, a health service and even a legislature fell into place. Some look back in anger, others with nostalgia.

All that changed again as the message sent out by Buddha and Ashoka, more than 2,000 years earlier, was taken up by a man named Gandhi. Once again, people listened and in 1947 the wheel turned a full circle as India returned to the Indians in the manner they had always claimed it—without bloodshed. Now they are carrying their wealth of history and legend into yet another millennium.

The nation was not forged in a day. Top: Akbar, the Great Mughal, brought many diverse lands together under his rule. Right: Today, India's proud soldiers march together on Independence Day as a symbol of the country's unity.

PART ONE

THE AWE-INSPIRING LANDSCAPE

Once upon a time, when the world was young, God asked the first man he was sending down to earth what kind of land he wanted to live on. Overwhelmed, the man burst out: "I want deep green valleys and snowy white mountains. I want fields of flowers and gushing rivers. I want endless deserts sands and deep blue seas. I want calm lakes and splashing rivers. I want..." So God sent him to India. It is not a single land at all, but a sprawling, colourful mosaic whose parts are indescribably different, irreconcilably individual. Like a string of diverse worlds.

The yak-tending shepherds of the Himalayas, who have spent their lives watching the sun sneak up from behind immense mountains, will tell you that India is frigid, fickle and flighty as the snow clouds. Or that it is harsh grey in one light and purple in the other. That its ethereal beauty turns almost sinister when the sun is going down and that nights are long and winters evil, but the sky is so close you can almost touch it.

Slide down the slopes of these giant mountains and you will find yourself in Kashmir. The hills are sprinkled with laughing flowers and, from a distance, the peaks seem friendly. Waterfalls gurgle down the rock and a mellow sun is set off against a brilliant blue lake.

Move southwest from here and the sunburnt people of Rajasthan will talk of the endless yellow and brown sprawl of the desert sands. Water is scarce and nothing survives except garishly-coloured cactus flowers. The sun is harsh and relentless but sometimes a gale blows, covering the sky with dust and nothing can be seen.

The rain-lashed farmers of Assam will tell you that India is grey and murky, its outlines are pastel and and its medium is water. They will describe a sky that is forever pouring and a land that is forever flooding.

But for much of India, especially along the Indo-Gangetic plain, green fields stretch out flat and endless—from the paddy plantations of Punjab to the sugar-cane farms of Uttar Pradesh and mile upon mile of wheat crop in Bihar.

Further south lies the Deccan Plateau, for most part an inhospitable scrubland dotted with tall spindly trees. But the monotony is broken up in startling colourful patches—bright wild sandalwood forests, grey ravines and deep-blue mountains.

Yet further south, the landscape changes again. The confusion of the plateau resolves into the vastness of the sea. The palm-fringed beaches seem to stretch on endlessly. Towards the furthest reaches of the peninsula, the grey waters of the Arabian Sea and the murky tides of the Bay of Bengal merge with the brilliant blue of the Indian Ocean.

The man who asked all this of God may have been greedy. But he chose well.

Nature dwarfs everything. Left: A pair of goat horns lies forlorn in the Zanskar mountains. Above: A devotee in Mahabalipuram is overwhelmed by the immensity of a holy rock. Preceding pages: Unspoilt by man the Rangdum Valley in Kashmir is surrounded by the lofty Himalayan ranges.

Thoughts of God soar in the mountains. Below: A string of prayer flags stretches to a temple in Leh, carrying the aspirations of humans heavenwards. Right: Some local artist has lovingly painted a smiling Buddha on a craggy rock in Ladakh. But journeys across this divine land are strewn with hazards. Preceding pages: An old man in Shey carefully negotiates a rock using his staff for better balance. Bottom: Younger people, however, make light of the same task in Matho, playfully leaping from rock to rock to get across a fast-flowing stream.

All along the Ladakh Himalayas, flat white structures dot the barren mountainsides (above, top left). Left: The sturdy Stok palace sprawls on the rock almost as if it had sprung from it.

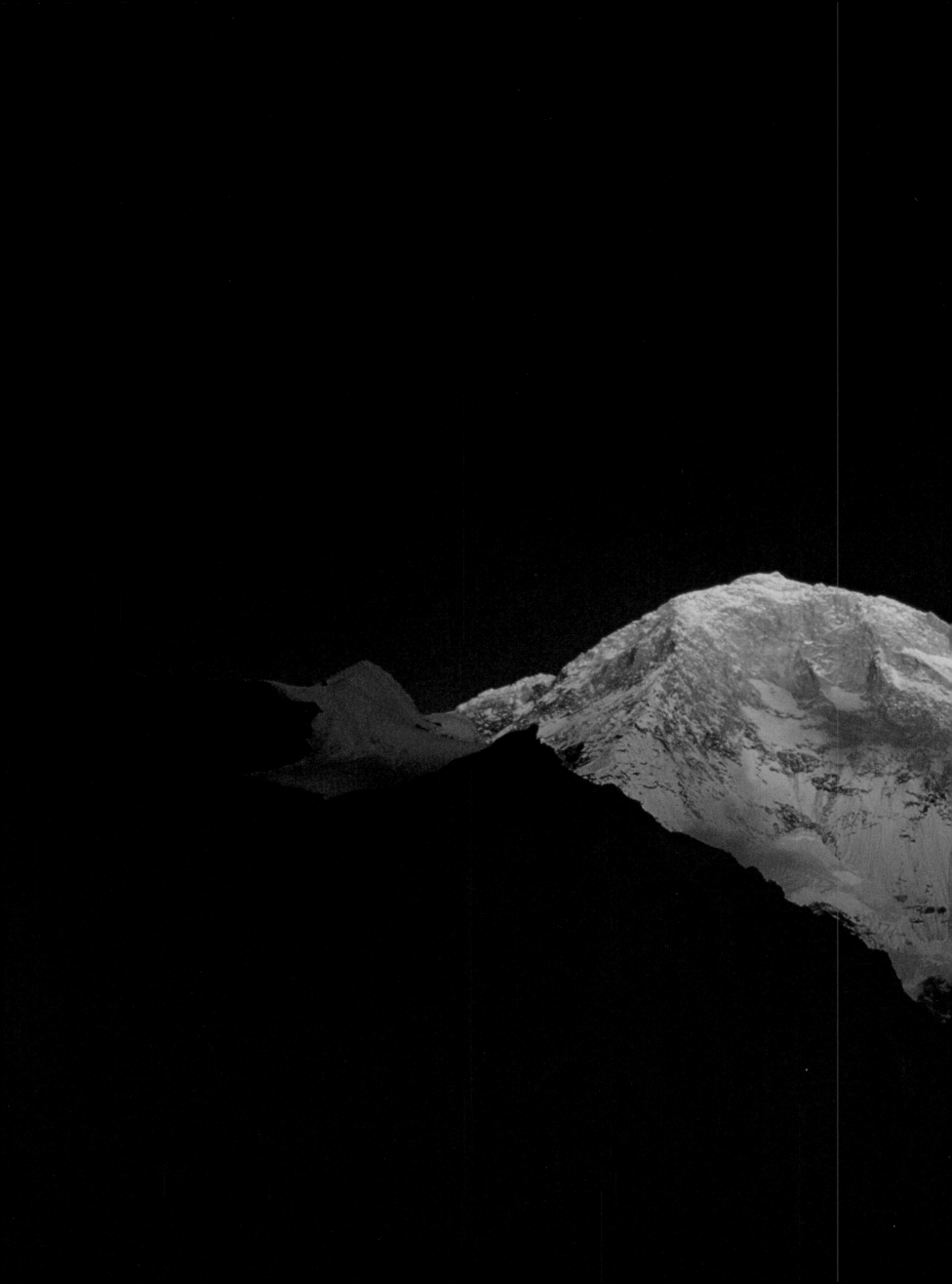

MOUNTAINS OF GOD

Northern India is dominated by mountains that are aloof as they are awe-inspiring. The immense Himalayas and the equally imposing Karakoram and Hindu Kush mountain ranges in the northwest can make you feel like a trespasser. Their vast cloak of snow runs for almost 3,000 kilometres, much of it unsullied by human print. Their peaks pierce the clouds and reach for the heavens. The sight of the 7,470-metre high Nanda Devi, surrounded by 70 other peaks glistening in the sun, is almost otherworldly.

No wonder the Hindus believe that the mountains are the source of all life, the abode of the gods "where Shiva lives and River Ganga falls from Vishnu's foot". Some of India's most revered pilgrimages are situated in the snow-clad mountains. Perhaps, people's thoughts turn to god when they see the Mt. Kanchenjunga rising a majestic 8,598 metres from a riotous valley of flowers.

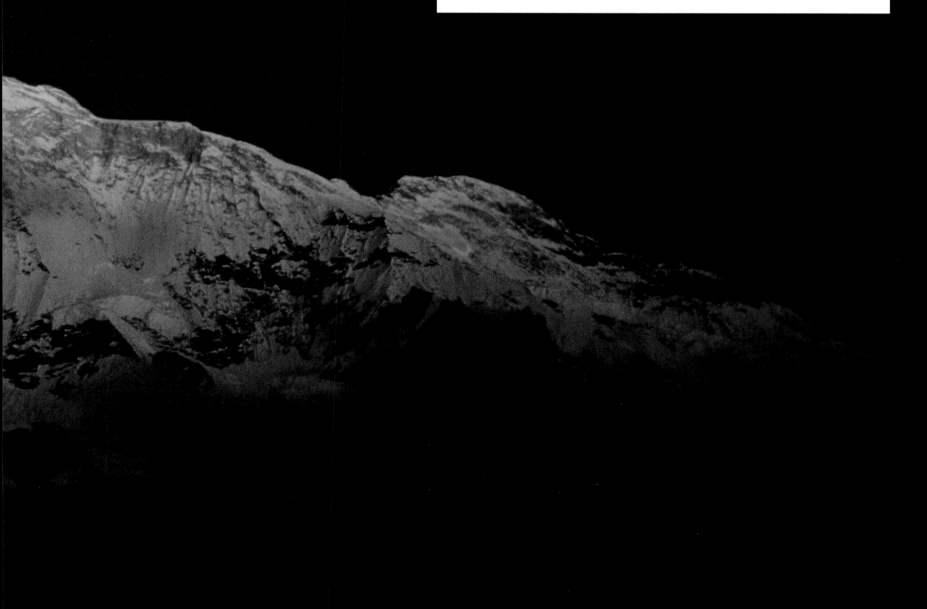

The magic grows with the day. Preceding pages: The first rays of the sun strike the Himalayas. Right: From a cave in Saspool, Ladakh, you can gaze—as if from a window—at India stretching out before you. Below: Kumzum Pass in Spiti is like a doorway through which one can enter the daunting Himalayas. Bottom: Bhaga river slices through rock to make such passes possible.

Passage to India

India is sealed from the rest of the world by the world's highest mountains. They form an imposing wall—eight kilometres high, 240 kilometres thick and almost 4,000 kilometres long. You would think that no one could breach this craggy, frigid barrier, and you would be wrong. Actually, this wall has secret entrances.

Mountain Passes

Over the centuries, melting snows have coursed down the mountains to form rivers. These, in turn, have gathered body and volume, eaten through rock and carved a series of passes for themselves. These passes, such as the Khyber and Zoji-La, were the original gateways through which migrants from all over Central Asia entered India, stayed on and formed the backbone of India's culture and civilisation

Breathtaking Beauty of the Hills

The mountains of India are aloof and desolate. Great blasts of heat rise from the world below. But somewhere between the two, perched on rolling hills or nestling in verdant valleys, lies a magical belt that some have called paradise. The flowers are forever in bloom, crisp breezes blow and at times you can hear the murmur of a waterfall or the splash of rivers in a hurry. This belt runs throughout the Hindu Kush and Himalayan foothills at altitudes between 1,000 and 3,000 metres. The jewel in its crown, the magical vale of Kashmir, has been known to the world since at least the 13th century. But other "hill towns" were discovered and developed by the British seeking to flee the heat of the plains. Till today, you find centres of military and administration in the hills of Shimla, Mussoorie and Dalhousie that were set up in colonial days.

Every summer, domestic tourists descend on these towns, seeking succour from the heat just as the British did before them. To beat this crunch, intrepid trekkers have started heading for still unexplored mountain hamlets. And they have struck gold. If anything, the sight of rhododendrons in bloom at the valley of flowers or the cherry blossoms and green slopes of Narkanda seem even more spectacular than the polished beauty of Mussoorie.

No one can remain untouched by the bounty nature has scattered.
Right: A woman smiles to herself amidst the mustard field that will bring food to her table.
Far Right: A little girl, with no such considerations, gets a whiff of a bloom.

Mountains are like magnets drawing visitors from the plains every summer.
Left: The lights of Shimla sparkle like a giant billboard advertising this hill resort.
Above: Houseboats at Kashmir's Nagin Lake wait to transport tourists to a world of dreams.

DESERT SANDS

Home in the desert is often a makeshift camp under an open sky.
Above: Home is where water is.
Right: This little girl, at left, at least has a thatch to live in.

The desert is a cruel place and the Thar Desert is harsher than most. Almost nothing grows in its sprawl of 200,000 square kilometres except stunted shrubs and straggly grasses. Moist winds heading towards the desert are turned away by the ancient Aravalli Range. Life is an endless quest for water as an entire year's rainfall does not exceed 10 centimetres. Most of the ground water is saline and useless. So when a few drops fall from the sky in June, people rush to store them in anything that is available such as tanks, tubs, buckets...but then the angry sun returns and temperatures rise past 50° C. Every scrap of moisture is sapped from the sand. And, as if to twist the knife, the winds start howling, blowing at speeds of up to 150 kilometres an hour, lifting up the sands and covering the land and sky with them. It is a miserable life, but the people of the desert have survived it for more than 2,000 years.

A Lifetime of Wandering

Many centuries ago, some people fled the harsh Thar Desert hoping to start a new life in a faraway land. Today, the world knows them as the wandering gypsies of Romania. Interestingly, even those who stayed behind in the Thar are always wandering, always on the road, like their blood brothers a continent away. These are the goatherds, moving from scrub to scrub in search of vegetation to feed their flock. Along with the *banjaras*, communities of wandering acrobats, these goatherds scour the sands with their camels and caravans. When night falls and desert temperatures drop suddenly, these nomads gather around campfires to sing ballads about times gone by. They sing of love and lovers. They sing of heroes who died fighting invaders. And they sing of rain falling on the sand. But it never rains.

There are no roads in the Thar and yet, people keep moving. Above: Goatherds and their flock search for food in Jaisalmer, kicking up gusts of dust in their wake. A herd can walk up to 20 kilometres a day under the searing sun.
Left: Camel carts wander for kilometres and wherever people finds fodder for their emaciated cattle, they wrap it up in little bundles.
Right: The monsoon winds pass tantalisingly close—just east of the Thar Desert—leaving the stretch from the Rann of Kutch to the Punjab plains devoid of rain.

The awkward, hunched, remorselessly overworked camels find themselves being pampered for a few days at Pushkar. Left: The camel trade, in seven days at Pushkar, is greater than the trade in the rest of the year put together. Thousands of camels await their new masters. Below: Camels are fed and fattened to impress customers. Right: A man shows off his purchase.

The Mother of All Fairs

Every year, for more than two millennia, thousands of people have been gathering at Pushkar for a spectacular marriage of religion, trade and entertainment. Pilgrims from all over India start converging on Pushkar some time in November to pray at the ancient temple of Brahma, the Creator. More than a hundred thousand of them pitch tents on the outskirts of this desert town and, on full moon day they head for a dip in the sacred lake of Pushkar. The water is near freezing as winters are cold in the desert. For more than a week, the evenings explode with centuries-old musicals, rides on ferris wheels and freak shows. There are wrestling matches and shows of strength. Meanwhile, the real business of the week is quietly taking place as traders have gathered to examine and buy millions of camels and cattle, specially bred for this occasion. It is not merely the oldest cattle fair in the world, it is also the largest.

There are just two or three temples dedicated to Brahma, the Creator, in all of India and Pushkar has the greatest one of all. Above all, the fair is a great pilgrimage.
Right: An old couple who have made the journey. Far right: Another pilgrim. Facing page: On full moon day, Kartik Poornima, pilgrims walk down the bathing steps into the winter-chilled waters of the lake.
Below: Stopping by at the waterhole.

Pushkar is also a celebration of life in the desert. Far left: Young girls at a Tivoli fair. Left: Rajasthan's folk dancers throb with exuberance and energy.

THE HEART OF THE LAND

T hree quarters of India lives in its half-million villages and dreams of paradise in shades of green—the shimmering green corns of wheat, the fading green acres of maize and the cheeky green miles of paddy. These fields are India's lifeblood and they, in turn, depend on water.

Everything hinges on the monsoons. In June, when the sun has baked the soil lifeless, all eyes turn towards the sky. Everyone, from the humblest farmer who sniffs for dampness in the air to the most senior bureaucrat with sophisticated meterological equipment, monitors the progress of the rain-winds from the west. The slightest shift in air currents, the smallest delay, can spell drought and disaster. Green corns can shrivel to brown. That's why in India, Indra, the Lord of the Seasons, is considered the mightiest of the gods.

Only slightly less powerful, but also considered holy, are the rivers that irrigate the fields, the Ganga, Yamuna, Cauvery and Mahanadi. The tiny southern state of Kerala alone has 44 rivers, all of them rain-fed, each of them revered. For most of India, there is no green without water, no paradise without green.

Women do much of the work in the fields. Right: A woman cutting wheat. Facing page: Women bend their backs to sow rice in a Bengal village. Above: A millet field.

Many farming techniques have remained untouched by time. Left: Farmers still use bullock carts to plough the land. Above: Threshing wheat in Goa is joyous labour. Overleaf: Drying chilli peppers in Rajasthan.

Rains (Pouring Joy)

The rains are more than a lifeline. They bring with them a celebration, a romance and a light-headedness that soars beyond the merely practical. The first showers are always spectacular. The colour of the light changes, the wind rattles windows and the peacock breaks into a jaunty, hopping dance. Many leaky, mud-thatched schools shut down for the day. Their whooping students spill onto the streets, tear sheets of paper from their notebooks and float little paper boats along ever-widening puddles. Temple priests pocket tidy sums of money for interceding with the gods while local bards sing whimsical songs about this season of love. But the mood can swing suddenly. Too much rain and water rises waist-high on city roads, stopping traffic. And flash floods can uproot entire villages in their wake.

Through most of India, the sweetest sound is the splash of water.
Top and centre: A stream gushes through rice fields in Goa while the Chambal River, Rajasthan's lifeline, overflows.
Above: In most villages, there are no taps and water comes only from the village well.

Cherrapunjee—Wet, Wet, Wet

In Meghalaya, a breathtakingly beautiful state of undulating hills, rolling grasslands and cascading waterfalls, lies Cherrapunjee, a hamlet where sunshine is rare. Cherrapunjee is a bit of a damp squib. The reason is simple enough. It rains non-stop for about 150 days a year in this cloudy, thinly-populated place that stands on the crest of the Khasi hills. They call it the world's wettest place. On a single day, July 10, 1952, it rained an astonishing 989.6 mm.

India does not have many waterways as many of its rivers rise up and dry with the monsoons. But in some places, boats remain the most effective mode of transport.
Left: In Alleppey, in southern India, canals run through the town and help to move grain and immigrant labour from point to point.
Overleaf: For centuries, boatmen have done roaring business along the mighty Ganges. But even more than trade, it is religion that is the main driving force here. Pilgrims hire boats to take them to the heart of the river, where they make their offerings. And in Varanasi, boats ferry the ashes of the dead to scatter them in the river.

Rivers—The Ganges

High on the Himalayas, in Gangotri, lies the fount of India's most sacred and important river—the Ganges. Devout Hindus will tell you that actually the river springs from Lord Shiva's head, flows through his tresses and thus becomes so pure and divine that mere contact with it can wash away your sins. A more practical reason for worshipping this river is that, for centuries, it has provided sustenance to a stretch of land running more than 2,000 kilometres across a fertile basin. Its waters have nourished the fields, provided waterways for boats and electricity to homes. To the simple people of this land, this translates into a gift of life. So they have woven myths around the river and even call it *Ganga Ma* (Mother Ganges). Many Hindus believe that they are guaranteed a passage to heaven only if their ashes are immersed in its waters. And every 14 years, millions of them gather along its banks for a holy dip in the largest ceremony on earth, the Kumbh Mela.

India's coastline is always humming with activity. Below: A fishwife strides purposefully from the sea. Right: Fishing boats preparing to set out yet again in Goa.

PASSAGE TO THE SEA

That ghostly hour, when night is departing but dawn has not quite arrived, sees the beaches of Kerala at their busiest. Swarms of fishermen, barefooted and bare-backed, are straining in unison to pull their weather-beaten wooden vessels into the sea. Scores of them take off with a swish of oars and a sway of patched-up nets. When a reddish sun finally appears, these boats will be mere specks on the horizon, venturing ever further in search of prawns and pomfrets. The sun will light up 5,600 kilometres of India's coastline to reveal palm-fringed beaches and the blue and grey waters of the three oceans that hem the land. In Goa, land of song and seafood, tourists will celebrate yet another day at seven of the most stunning beaches in the world. In sacred Puri, pilgrims will hurl coins into the muddy waters of the ocean and watch open-mouthed as little urchins dive in to retrieve them. In Madras, people will sunbathe but not swim in the shark-infested waters. The tide will recede a full eight kilometres at Chandipur-on-Sea. Giant Ridley turtles will cover every grain of land near Bhubaneshwar. And just before the sun sets and the fishermen make their way back, waves will leap 40 metres in the air before settling on the white sands of Gopalpur.

India's waters are crammed with fish. Above: A fisherman's face cracks into a wide grin as he shows off his catch. Right: Boats take a breather while the fishwife's basket is full. Facing page: In Goa, a group of fishermen strain their backs to haul in the catch that has been snared by their nets.

The shimmering beauty of the sea comes alive in that twilight hour. Left: The sun is about to drop into a fisherman's net in Cochin. Far left: In the island of Rameshwaram, which was torn away from the mainland during a 15th century cyclone, the last rays of the sun wash the land red.

PART TWO

FLORA AND FAUNA

I t is, perhaps, no coincidence that the greatest wildlife tale of all time was inspired by India and set in its forests. You can still catch the magic and the mood of Rudyard Kipling's *The Jungle Book* in the dense and daunting jungles of Madhya Pradesh. Characters like Baloo the Bear, Sher Khan the Lion and Colonel Haathi the Elephant (all of which draw their names from Hindi) still stalk the land.

Of course, India crams many more species than Kipling could possibly capture in his classic. Its procession of more than 350 species of mammals ranges from bounding deer that leap more than four metres high to the snorting snow leopards and the one-horned rhinos that wallow in the swamps of Assam. Perhaps, only Africa can boast of a greater variety of life.

But one important change has taken place since the days of Kipling. In his masterpiece, it was the hapless human who was at the mercy of the beasts—endangered by the hunger of some and protected by the kindness of others. Now the pendulum has swung and it is the animals who are battling for survival.

The original culprits were the maharajahs, whose domains included jungles and forests. Their favourite pastime was to take their guests on massive hunting expeditions, in which bullets were rained on animals from the safety of a high perch. No one could hunt without the maharajah's sanction, which perhaps contained the damage a bit. It was after India gained independence in 1947, when the power of the maharajahs waned and the new government had not yet filled the void, that the real slaughter of the innocents took place. Whole species were wiped out during a three-year period in which it was open season for every stray hunter. The pink-headed duck has vanished altogether. There are now less than 2,000 musk deer left.

Again, in a neat reversal of *The Jungle Book* theme, man is now protector as well as predator. Some animals, such as the chattering monkeys and the lumbering bulls, both reputed to be helpers of god, are preserved by tradition. The government has stepped in to save some others from the brink of extinction by setting up national parks and wildlife sanctuaries for them. Hunting of certain species has been explicitly banned while others are being consciously bred to boost their numbers. Wildlife is beginning to perk up again.

The fields and forests, too, have weathered the assault of the woodcutter's axe. For a while it seemed they might vanish as a booming population and pressure on land led to the large-scale chopping down of trees. Feisty environmentalists have succeeded in stemming the tide and a bewildering variety of vegetation is blossoming again. The Jungle Book is coming back to life.

The fascination with the cheetah (above) stemmed from its reputation as the quickest of predators. Some hunters trained it to chase down prey while others shot it down. The cheetah is extinct. Will the tiger (left), go the same way?

FACE OF THE PREDATOR

India's jungles are neither gentle nor safe. Death can come suddenly and swiftly as the ruthless Royal Bengal Tiger, the agile panther and the wide-jawed, sharp-toothed clouded leopard lurk at unexpected corners. Make no mistake. They are some of nature's most efficient killing machines. As darkness descends on the jungle, these cats start roaming the territories they have marked out for themselves. Sometimes they hunt in packs, making a frontal attack on large prey, surrounding them from every direction and tearing out chunks of flesh from them while they are still alive. At other times, a solitary tiger sets up a silent ambush, waiting for hours for its victim to come within range. When it makes its move with a low growl and a quick pounce, there is no escape. Ironically, the reputation of these beasts as supreme killers has made them prime targets for anyone seeking to assert his machismo. The cheetah, that fleet-footed cat which once roamed India in its thousands, is now extinct. The last three were killed in 1948. The population of the tiger fell from 40,000 at the turn of the century to 1,827 in 1972. Careful preservation has pushed it back to 4,000 now. And the Asiatic Lion, which was once found all over the country is now restricted to a small pocket in a single forest. The magnificent predators stand cornered.

Few animals can face the fangs of these murderous beasts. Still, tigers and panthers prefer to hunt only the younger, smaller ones for their food. Facing page, bottom: The tiger, normally a nocturnal animal, has changed its habits due to shortage of prey. It now hunts in daylight as well. Facing page, top: The panther is a good climber and displays amazing strength of jaw as it bears away its prey.

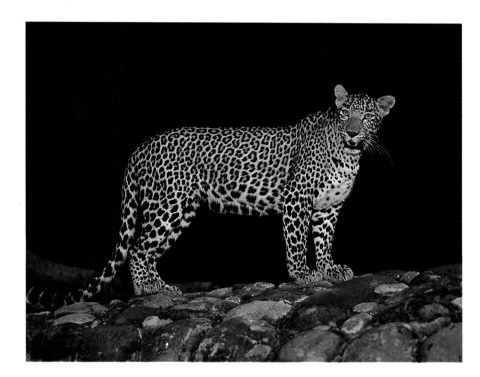

*As their habitats shrink and sources of water dry up, many jungle cats virtually camp beside waterholes when they find them. Below: A tigress with her cubs frolicking in a pool. Facing page: Tigers, which are excellent swimmers, love to take long leisurely dips.
Overleaf: A pride of lions in the Gir forests quench their thirst.*

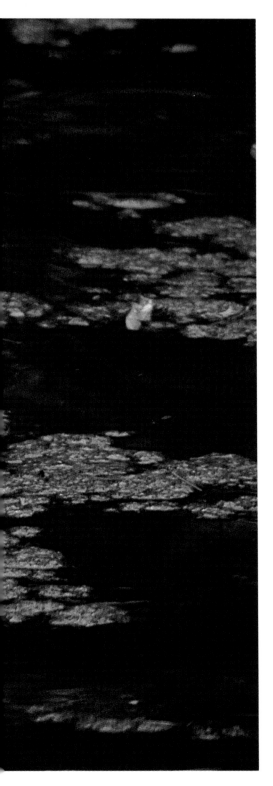

The Man-Eaters

A strange set of circumstances has produced the most fearsome beast of the jungle: the man-eater. Normally, tigers and lions do not eat man. But when age or injury slows them down, or when broken canines blunt their hunting skills, these animals seek out soft targets. And, as luck would have it, the shrinking jungles have brought them almost next door to humans who cannot run very fast or smell very acutely. These man-eaters often slink into the villages adjoining their forests at night and bear away their victims. Big game hunter Jim Corbett said that if a tiger gets addicted to the flesh of man, it never reforms. Once a tiger is declared a man-eater, plaster casts of its pug-marks are made and orders are issued to gun it down. Under Indian law, this is the only circumstance in which a tiger can be killed.

Village of Widows

Around the dense and forbidding mangrove forests of the Sunderbans stands one of the saddest villages in India. Most women wear white—the colour traditionally worn by a Hindu widow. Vidhabapalli (literally "village of widows") is home to more than 150 women whose husbands have been slain by the Royal Bengal Tiger. The tragedy of the village is that many of its men are honey-collectors, who go deep into the forest to search for honeycombs. There lurks the Royal Bengal Tiger, a peculiar species that has turned man-eater because of starvation, not disability. There are not enough animals in the forest to sustain the tiger population. In any case, the swampy marshes that run through the forest make it difficult for it to chase after fast-moving prey. So it turns upon the poor honey-collectors and leaves behind an entire community of grieving wives.

Lord of the Jungle

The villages around the Gir forests of Gujarat have strange neighbours. More than 205 Asiatic Lions, the last surviving members of their species, lazily wander in and out of these villages, where people have got used to them. In fact, every one of these lions has been given its own individual name by the villagers. And every evening, the villagers rake in a few more rupees by arranging "lion shows" for the tourists. They attract the lions in the forest by tethering a goat or sheep to a tree. Invariably, an ageing beast, too tired to hunt, or a pregnant lioness makes its way to the spot, while the wide-eyed tourists gawk from some 500 metres away. Of course the lions are not always such good neighbours. They are not man-eaters but sometimes, even when there are no shows taking place, they sneak into the village and drag away the occasional sheep or buffalo.

Treating the King

When a lion injures itself, do you just sit back and watch it die? The villagers around Gir have invented ingenious methods to treat it. They tether a goat to a tree and wait in its branches for the injured lion to show up. In their hands is a five-metre wooden pole, with a medicine-laden cloth tied at one end. While the lion is busy slaughtering the bait, the villagers use the pole to clean its wounds. The operation is repeated until the inflammation goes away. And if they want a sick lion to ingest some medicine, they merely inject it into the liver of a slain goat and wait for the lion to eat it. It is a medical scheme fit for a king.

REPTILES—SLIMY, SLITHERY, SACRED

On the one hand, no species is venerated more in India than the curling, wriggling, slithering snakes. On the other, no species is feared more. Perhaps, they are revered precisely because they are so fearsome—snake bites cause more than 10,000 deaths in the country every year as people move barefoot in a land teeming with reptiles. And among its 200 species of snakes, India can count the deadly kraits, vipers and cobras and the even deadlier king cobras. Yet the snakes are seen as companions of the gods. Lord Shiva wears the cobra as a garland around his neck while Hindus believe that the king of serpents was used as a rope to churn the ocean and retrieve the nectar of the gods. One still finds wandering devotees of Shiva trundling along with snakes around their necks. It is a typically Indian paradox that these same snakes are also hunted down in their millions so that their skins can be exported. The problem grew so acute that the government had to clamp an official ban on such exports. But an illegal trade still flourishes and one tribe in Tamil Nadu depends so much on it that its men have taken up no other occupation.

Naag Panchami, the Festival of Serpents (above), comes to India every year with a massive snaring of cobras. These are then taken to the hundreds of snake temples across the country, where devotees feed them milk—and think this makes them immune to snake bite.
Right: A young tribal handles a vine snake.

Ultimate War Machine

Snakes are among the most efficient of predators. They can move fast and strike with blinding speed. The more poisonous among them, like the king cobra, emit venom that can kill within 25 minutes. Cobras can also "spit" their venom up to distances of 2.5 metres and blind their prey. The non-poisonous snakes are no less formidable. They have elastic jaws that can stretch unbelievably to let them swallow prey several times the size of their mouth. They have slim bodies that let them lie in ambush inconspicuously. And they have a slow metabolism that enables them to wait for days, even weeks, for the right prey to come within striking distance.

Snakes can be playmates too.
Above: The deadly king cobra in a snake handler's basket.
Right: A snake charmer "kisses" a snake and sometimes gets high on its venom.

The fascination with the python (right) stems from its sheer size. The largest of these snakes can grow up to 11 metres. They have known to crush a man-sized prey to death and swallow it whole. Ironically, these fierce creatures are devoted parents and actually brood their eggs like a hen.

Snake Charmers

It is one of India's lasting images. A man blows on a bloated pipe while a serpent, its hood erect and its eyes transfixed, dances before him. Charming snakes in India is not merely an art, it is a way of life.
For centuries, entire tribes and villages have done nothing except catch snakes and handle them. The myth is that these snakes are de-fanged, but that is not really true. The snake charmers start handling snakes from the age of six. They use their pipes the way a conductor uses his baton to make the snake sway and twirl with them. Traditional snake charmers think they have taken the snake on loan from god. They take a vow to release every snake within six months on pain of being bitten.

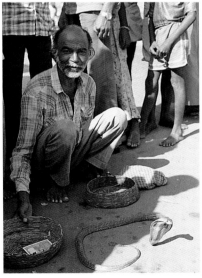

Snake shows are among the most common form of entertainment in India. Left: Snake charmers have developed quaint snake dances in which they wriggle and sway like serpents. As newer pastimes emerge, snake charmers struggle to eke out a living.

51

NATIONAL PARKS

A s India's forest cover started dwindling and its species of birds and mammals began to vanish, the policy-makers decided there was only one way to preserve the variety of life. Certain areas were marked out as the exclusive domain of animals. No hunting, farming, grazing or felling of trees is allowed within these boundaries. Right now, India's 75 national parks, 421 wildlife sanctuaries and 35 zoological gardens cover more than 130,000 square kilometres or about 4.5 per cent of the land between them. Inside is preserved the most exotic and endangered of India's wildlife. The rare snow leopard, the ibex, the 12-antlered deer, the one-horned rhinoceros, the gibbon, the tusker and even the crocodiles along the Ganges—all have found safe havens within these parks. But success creates its own problems. As animals within these forests multiply, they find that the parks are not big enough to support them. And if they spill over into the villages, they are ensnared or gunned down. This creates contant friction between the wildlife officials, zealously protecting their beasts, and the villagers who are always on the lookout for fresh meat.

Some animals have all the luck.
Right: As servants of Lord Rama, monkeys are revered, safe from people, and even have temples in their honour.
Above: A snow leopard is not so lucky and is gradually disappearing.

The cheetal (above), with its distinctive white spots, is India's most beautiful and abundant deer. It moves in large herds, up to several hundred strong. These herds become easy targets for tigers and panthers. But the cheetal population is in no danger, multiplying as it does, giving birth twice a year.

Despite the protection they get at national parks, many species are facing extinction. The black buck (right), one of the fastest runners in the animal world, cannot outrun poachers' bullets. The langur, a black-faced monkey (centre, left), is sometimes captured to entertain villagers. Centre, right: The wild gaur, a bison-like creature that can grow up to 1,000 kilograms, is often too formidable to hunt.
Centre, below: The beautiful Periyar Wildlife Sanctuary thrives around a man-made lake, nurturing hordes of elephants, macaques and squirrels.
Bottom, left: The gharial, a crocodilia found only in India, is hunted for its tough and durable hide. It can grow up to seven metres. Bottom, right: A Travancore tortoise.

Rhinos of Kaziranga

Even in their last refuge in the jungles of Assam, the one-horned rhinoceroses are under constant attack—from nature, man and themselves. Every year when the rains come, about two-thirds of the Kaziranga National Park gets flooded and the rhinos have to run for high land. Defenceless outside their sanctuary, these massive 2,000-kilogram creatures are hunted for the horn which protrudes from their snout. Their horn symbolises the lingam, male sexual organ, and is said to contain powerful aphrodisiac qualities. And once they have survived the rains and the killers, the rhinos suddenly realise that the limpid pools and grazing grounds of the park are too small for their 2,000-strong population. So they fight for space. They disable each other in vicious duels. But with all its problems, the Kaziranga National Park has at least sustained the last of these rhinoceroses, when other havens have dried up.

A one-horned rhino (above) wallows in a pool at Kaziranga. A full-grown adult can weigh up to 2,000 kilograms. It is a fierce beast, attacking even elephants with its tusks and sending them scurrying for shelter. Its weapon is not a weapon of war. It is ornamental.

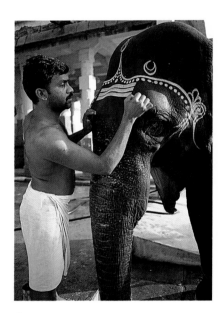

Legend has it that when Lord Shiva accidentally lopped off his son's head, he replaced it with the head of an elephant. Thus Ganesha, the elephant-headed god was born. Since then, the elephant itself has become an object of veneration. Above: Many elephants are bred at temples for worship. Here, one of them gets dolled up before a ceremony. Right: An elephant gambolling in the wild. Even their revered status cannot save them from poachers.

Elephants make wonderful students. They are intelligent and can easily be trained to do man's bidding.
Left: Elephants are in great demand at the circus where they perform titillating tricks.
Right: In Periyar, elephants are sometimes trained to lift logs that choke waterways. Below, right: The royal families of Rajasthan have always maintained elephants—for carrying them to war and bearing them to happier occasions like weddings.

Elephants Everywhere

Occasionally, at busy street intersections, among cars and buses, you can find a massive elephant swishing its tail and waiting for the traffic signal to turn green. No one bats an eyelid. The elephant is as much a part of India as the Taj or the Ganges. Over the centuries it has been treated, alternately, as an animal of war, a vehicle for the hunt, a beast of burden and a messenger of the gods. Now city-dwellers have no use for it and, in any case, few can afford its daily diet of 300 kilograms of fodder. So the elephant has returned where it came from—the nature reserves of Assam, Kerala and Uttar Pradesh. There the herd gambols in deep pools of water. And there it hides from poachers who chase it for its 50-kilogram tusks.

Climbing with the Yaks

At altitudes above 4,000 metres, where water freezes in winter and very little grows, lives an animal which the locals seem to have specially ordered from heaven. God knows what the people of northern Ladakh would have done without the wild yak, a massive, bison-like animal. It ploughs their land. Its milk feeds their children. Its hide turns back the cold and its dung is used as fuel. And when the people want to make a journey to still higher regions, the yak makes an excellent porter. It never stumbles and one does not even have to find water for it. It feeds on snow.

BIRDS—FLYING HIGH

India must have the noisiest and nosiest birds in the world. They start chattering before the break of dawn. They dart into apartment blocks and try to build their nests in lofts and on cupboards. They dirty car tops and shamelessly demand grain from the villagers. There are 1,200 species of them, each staking its claim on a piece of sky. Many of them get cheeky in the knowledge that they are protected by tradition.

The sarus crane, so faithful that it never takes another partner even after its mate is dead, symbolises a happy marriage throughout India. The brilliantly plumed peacock is a harbinger of the monsoons. Swans are companions of the gods. Then there are other birds that need no protection. The powerful, broad-shouldered falcon, with its white breast and cruel eyes, is itself a deadly killer. Rich sheiks often buy it and train it to swoop from the sky and hunt other birds for them. Killers and prey—and all other birds in between—gather around India's lakes and pools, have angry disputes over territory and often a single tree winds up with nests of 10 different species. As if India's own birds were not enough, it attracts more than 300 species of migratory birds, who flee the cold of their lands and add their own chirps to the carnival.

The painted stork (above) is a wonderful hunter and a good parent. It spreads its wings like a parasol to save its chicks from the heat. Right: The painted wood stork in flight, looking for worms and fish.

The monal, an outrageously colourful bird (left), is hunted for its bright crest and feathers. Below: The Great Indian bustard can grow up to a metre in height and weigh 20 kilograms. It is on the verge of extinction.

The brilliant peacock (left) has been declared India's national bird. When it spreads its wings and dances, farmers rejoice because it means rains are around the corner. The sight of a male cavorting is a joy by itself.

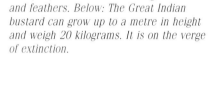

Siberian Cranes

They are India's best-known and most regular tourists. They arrive punctually every Christmas, covering a 6,400-kilometre journey from the freezing farms of Siberia to the friendly forests of Bharatpur Bird Sanctuary, about 200 kilometres from New Delhi. Then this tall, happy bird, which is fighting for survival, immediately gets into the spirit of the season, fluttering its wings, ruffling its feathers, raising its long neck, emitting a cry, throwing out its chest and breaking into a funny, frenzied dance.

IN BLOOM

A botanist could go mad in India. If he spent just a single day studying each different species of plant blossoming there, it would still take him two lifetimes to get through the list. The country is home to 45,000 different species of vegetation, 35 per cent of which are unique to Indian soil. The rarest of these are ancient herbs, tapped for medicine, that sprout in jungles so dense that light never quite trickles down to the undergrowth.

But the most spectacular plants bloom in the Himalayas. At altitudes of 5,000 metres, way above the treeline, are small, brilliantly coloured flowers, many of which have no name. Come down a little and there are miles upon miles of white laurels, maples, alders, birches, conifers and junipers. Forests of bamboo and willow jostle each other on the lower reaches. But nothing quite matches the riot of colour in the eastern Himalayas, one of the wettest regions in the world, where no less than 4,000 species of plant, including the orchid, magnolia, rhododendron and primula, dance against the backdrop of stunning snow peaks in what must be the world's highest valley of flowers.

India's mountains are home to an array of spectacular blooms. Some, among them, are highly sought after for their medicinal value. Ayurveda, the traditional Indian system of medicine, is based entirely on extracts of herbs that flower in the Himalayas or the jungles.
Top right: Gloriosa superba, a plant known for its medicinal value. The plants on the hills can be beautiful as they are useful.
Top: Berries among thorn thickets in Ladakh. Above: An apricot orchard in Ladakh. Right: A mustard field.

The saffron fields of Kashmir (below) are unique. It is among a handful of places on earth where they thrive.
Bottom: Some of the bushes in these plantations are 200 years old.
Right: The pine forests of Kashmir.

Mushrooms (above) whet appetites and bank balances.
Overleaf: The sunflower fields of Karnataka yield oil and livelihoods.

Fields of Dreams

Some of India's most beautiful scenery never changes and some of its prettiest plants replicate themselves endlessly, stretching out in fields as far as the eye can see. Deep in the north lie the flashy saffron fields of Pampore, one of the few places in the world where saffron is grown. On the eastern reaches in Assam is an unending carpet of green as 750 tea-gardens stand shoulder to shoulder, their brilliant colours occasionally softened by clouds. And towards the south of the country, in Andhra Pradesh, yellow is the colour of the landscape as the world's largest sunflower fields leave no room for anything else.

PART THREE
PEOPLE, CUSTOMS AND BELIEFS

A student who has never been to India might be forgiven for thinking that he can learn about the place merely by memorising a few salient facts from textbooks: that it is a country obsessed with religion, having given birth to Hinduism, Buddhism, Jainism and Sikhism and played host to Islam and Christianity; that its people are dark, poor, illiterate and steeped in exotic tradition; that it is a land of yoga, vegetarianism and the caste system.

It is only when you step inside the country that you realise that perhaps no six letters can stretch farther or hide more than I-N-D-I-A-N. The word stands for so many clashing, contrasting, conflicting elements that you wonder if it means anything at all. The diversity—in dress, dialect, diet and demeanour—is mind-boggling.

The differences leap out and strike you even at first glance. The faces that you see might be fair or dark or any complexion in between. The races may differ. The voices that resonate in the air could be speaking in any of 700 languages and dialects. Even the length of cloth that men swathe around their waist and the saree that women wear might be tied in any of a dozen distinct ways.

Scratch the surface and the differences seem to widen even further. True, 80 per cent of the country is Hindu, but that is neither here nor there. Every region has cut the loose fabric of the religion to fit its own needs. Every village has fashioned its own customs. To complicate matters further, an ancient and uniquely Indian system has divided the society into innumerable castes and sub-castes.

The caste system started out 3,000 years ago as a way of classifying people according to their hereditary occupations. But over the years, it degenerated into a rigid pecking order in which, even till a few years back, a high-caste Brahmin would feel "polluted" simply because an outcaste's shadow had fallen on him. Thankfully, the system has now eased its grip and communities that were once relegated to the sidelines of society are now a vigorous and integral part of it. But centuries of apartness have left behind one interesting legacy. Today, there are more than 4,200 distinct communities in India. Their ways are so diverse that, as Indians learn more about each other's practices, they often go wide-eyed with amazement.

The austere Jains, with their reverence for all things living, shun meat, eggs and even onions. Some cover their mouths with pieces of cloth so that their breathing might not inadvertently harm the miniscule germs and bacteria floating in the air. Imagine their bewilderment on running into the rat-eating Musahir tribe of Bihar, or the crocodile-chomping river people of Karnataka.

But sometimes these differences dissolve in a celebration of life and tradition. India's scores of festivals bring its people together in a mass fervour that others can only gape at. Complete strangers embrace and dance on the streets. And perhaps, the student who had tried to learn of India from his textbooks is left wondering how so much camaraderie can co-exist with so much diversity.

A South Indian family gazes at the horizon (left). Above: The confident faces of schoolchildren peering into their future.

63

FACES OF INDIA

An artist, attempting to put on canvas the portrait of a typical Indian, will tell you there is no such thing. Look north and you find the delicate Kashmiris with their almost Caucasian complexions and large, light eyes. Look south, and you find the ebony-hued Tamil speakers with thick, curly hair and dark flashing eyes. In the northeast there live a clutch of Mongoloid races, slant-eyed, high-cheeked, their figures squat and powerful. They are equally at home with spears and guitars. In the west, around the Gir forests of Gujarat, live the Siddhis, unadulterated Negroids who still follow the customs of their African ancestors and are reputed to have come to India along with the lions who walk the jungles. Scattered in between are the snub-nosed, bare-bodied tribal women of Bastar, the cloaked and veiled Muslim ladies from Lucknow and the tall, scowling, moustachioed men of Rajasthan. There is no common denominator. Even the way they wear their hair is different. The burly Sikhs, their faces framed by handsome beards, let their hair grow all the way down to their waist but tie it up in turbans. The sadhus, wandering mendicants, let loose matted locks fall down their backs while the Brahmins of Kerala tonsure their scalps until the sunlight bounces off them. So which of them is a typical Indian? All of them.

With many people clinging to the villages where they were born, most Indians never get to experience the diverse sprinkling of races in their country.
Above: A woman from southern sunny Andhra Pradesh, her tanned skin glistening, laughs with the exuberance of youth. Right: An old man from a Mongoloid hill tribe in the north gazes pensively at the onset of winter.
Below: Temples, like this one in Goa, are a meeting point for Hindus of all denominations..
Bottom: Hindu girls from Varanasi.

Topography, history and sometimes religion ensure that a strong strand of sharing overlays the differences between communities.
Facing Page (top row, left to right): The chill of the Himalayas and the message of Buddhism bring together this old woman from Zanskar, this Kashmiri from Leh and the lady gazing out from her window in Ladakh. (Second row): They are all creatures of the desert—the mother and child from Jaisalmer, the handsome Rajput and the laughing beauty. (Third row): The faces may look different but all these women worship the same Hindu deities. (Fourth row): Religion can divide too. This Sikh is a non-smoker while the old woman, whose religion does not place such restrictions on her, puffs away. The fisherman from Goa does not care.

TRIBALS—PEOPLE FROM ANOTHER TIME

They are people of the forest and the river, whose origins are lost in the mists of time. India's aboriginal tribals, who number more than 100 million, dot almost every part of the country. They are determined to preserve the ways of their ancestors. In some cases they are openly distrustful of outsiders, chasing them away with arrows and blowpipes. Other tribes accept government grants and jobs but still stick to their customs. The Murias of Madhya Pradesh, for example, still run dormitories in which their teenagers can get to know each other, away from the supervision of their elders. Then there are other tribes, like the Gonds, who sanction only marriage by elopement. The couple has to run away and hide in the forest, living off the land. Their marriage is sanctified only if they can give their pursuers, the girl's kin, the dodge. And in Rajasthan, there are tribes of hereditary robbers, who can still be found in many jails of the state. Most tribes still worship their ancient gods of tree and fire and try to scrape together a living from hunting and primitive agriculture. Poverty, however, is inducing others to head for the cities.

Poverty may have robbed them of much else, but some tribes continue to dress as flamboyantly as their forefathers. Women wear colours of fertility, their beads are a status symbol, the bangles up to their elbow denote marriage and the elaborate mirrorwork of their handprinted skirts is a sign of prosperity.
Above: A tribal from Pushkar.
Right: Hampi tribals try to make ends meet in an alien city environment.

To help tribals catch up economically with the rest of the country, 7.5 per cent of all government jobs are reserved for them. But these quotas often lapse as there are not enough qualified tribal applicants for these jobs. Meanwhile people from these tribes eke out a living doing manual labour.
Right: An impoverished tribal woman from Karnataka. Far right: A lode-picker from Rajasthan.

The Banjara or gypsy tribes have consistently turned down government employment, preferring instead to earn their living as "Nats" (dancers) or high-wire acrobats. Their caravans keep travelling in search of an audience. Above: Three generations of women from the Banjara tribe, whose lives have remained unchanged for centuries.

CHILDREN OF MANY GODS

There must be something about India that makes man's thoughts turn to god. Five thousand years back, when religion probably had no name, images of the Mother Goddess were being fashioned along the bank of the River Indus. It took another 1,500 years before Hinduism took root. It was a comprehensive religion, telling its followers how to lead their lives, urging them to do their duty and assuring them that they would be rewarded for it. Nearly all of India took it up until, in the 6th century B.C., two great men—Buddha and Mahavira—gave the country other creeds to choose from. Buddhism spread far beyond India's shores while Jainism, a faith of compassion and non-violence, retains thousands of followers even today. Christianity came to India as early as A.D. 50 through St Thomas and immediately won some followers in Kerala. Judaism followed 20 years later. A thousand years after this, the soldiers of Islam conquered large parts of India and many Indians, especially those disillusioned with the caste system, started converting to it. India even added its own touch to Islam through the cult of Sufis, wandering mendicants who preached a gentle faith about brotherhood of man. Just when one thought that the country's religious canvas could hold no more, it gave birth to Sikhism. Zoroastrianism, Bahaism and many denominations of Christianity also carved out their niches. Though 83 per cent of India is Hindu today, the gods of its dozens of other faiths also keep watch on the country.

There is room for every form of divinity in India. Top: A Sikh devotee says his prayers at the Golden Temple.
Above: Catholics hold a Palm Sunday service in palm-fringed Goa.
Far left: Jains pour milk at the feet of the 18 metres statue of their saint Bahubali.
Left: A wandering Sufi, on the other hand, does not believe in idol worship.
Facing page: Buddhists light candles in Bodhgaya, where Buddha received enlightenment.

Ritually-Right Hindus

Ever since it took root, some 1,500 years before the birth of Christ, Hinduism started inventing rituals and deities. As of now, the religion recognises some 330 million deities, many of them known only by a few villages or families.

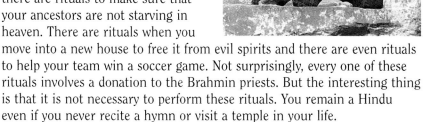

The Brahmins, interpreters of Hinduism, insisted upon elaborate rituals that only they could perform. This added to their power. Even today, there are rituals to make sure that your ancestors are not starving in heaven. There are rituals when you move into a new house to free it from evil spirits and there are even rituals to help your team win a soccer game. Not surprisingly, every one of these rituals involves a donation to the Brahmin priests. But the interesting thing is that it is not necessary to perform these rituals. You remain a Hindu even if you never recite a hymn or visit a temple in your life.

Most Hindus, however, choose the middle path. Basic rituals are observed. Other than that, each home has a clutch of idols and portraits of deities. And each Hindu family tries to visit a temple at least once a week, announcing its presence with a ringing of bells and an offering of flowers. The chant of hymns, the beat of cymbals and the glow of lamps from these shrines drift through the night, spreading the warmth of this easygoing religion.

Hindus believe that out of 16 possible offerings to God, flowers are the most sacred. Above: Tons of marigolds wind up every day at the Shiva temple in Jhalwar. Above right: In exotic Khajuraho, a bright red flower is offered to Ganesha, the God of auspicious beginnings.

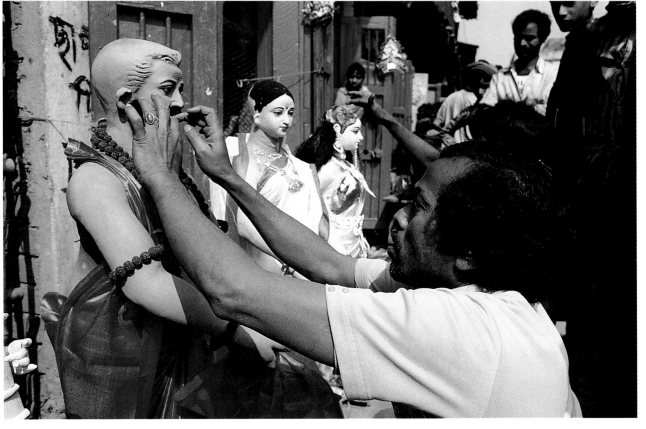

*The language of Hinduism is rich with symbols.
Facing page: An old man pouring water in the direction of the sun believes that this will quench the thirst of his forefathers in heaven.
Left: A baby being initiated into the ways of his religion is showered with coins so that Lakshmi, the Goddess of Wealth, will always smile upon him.
Above: Lovingly carved images of deities are believed to be imbued with the spirits of the gods themselves.*

Varanasi or Benares is known as the city of light. To Hindus it is also the city of death. They believe that many millennia ago, Lord Shiva burst through Varanasi as a blaze of light that stretched from earth to heaven. Hindus therefore believe that dying in Varanasi assures them a passage to heaven. Even if they can't die here, Hindus want their ashes to be immersed in the Ganga waters of this holy city. That is why widows and orphans from every corner of India flock to Varanasi with the remains of their loved ones. A complex ritual follows. Priests who specialise in funeral rites orchestrate ceremonies on the banks of the river. People then walk down the ghats—stepped landings that lead to the Ganges—and take a dip in its waters. The ashes are then allowed to float into eternity.
Preceding pages: Crowds on the ghats cleanse themselves in the Ganges. Left: Three men perform funeral rites and say final goodbyes to a loved one.
Below: A cremation by the river.

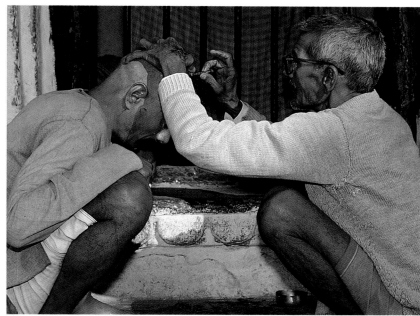

Varanasi is also the city of Lord Vishwanath, Overlord of the Universe. A visit to his temple and a sacrifice of something personal and precious is said to ensure salvation and break the cycle of death and rebirth. Left: People shave off hair, which has great spiritual significance in Hinduism, and offer it to Lord Vishwanath as a sign of their devotion. Below: Devotees take a dip in the Ganges. This custom has been prevalent since the first millennium B.C.

To call attention to themselves, pilgrims have to follow certain rituals in the presence of the deity. Facing page: At Airateshwara Temple in Tamil Nadu, a devotee sounds a bell to rouse the deity from his slumber. Right: Men chant hymns in the praise of the Lord. Left: After the deity has heard human prayers, a sacred flame is lit in his presence. The devotee then places his outstretched palm a few centimetres above the flame. This is supposed to transport the blessings from the deity to you— and it means that your prayer will be heard.

Pilgrims of the Soul

Every Hindu is allowed to make personal deals with his favourite deity: Fulfil my heartfelt desire, he says, and I will cross rivers and mountains to offer my prayers at your abode. Hindus are convinced that these deities actually live among them, listening to their prayers and problems. Many such abodes of god nestle on steep hills. Some devotees actually walk barefoot up the rocky slopes to petition their deities or to thank them for wishes granted. They treat the pilgrimage as a form of penance. Of course, the more arduous the journey, the more the devotee expects to be rewarded for it.

Half the joy of pilgrimage is the process of getting there. Far left: An entire family, with its idols and children, has set off in a bullock cart to worship a deity in Soundatti. Above: The old and the infirm are forgiven if they ride piggyback or get carried in chairs to the Jain temple in Sravanabelagola. Left: An elephant blesses a devotee in Tamil Nadu.

Sadhus

Hinduism is said to have been invented by *rishis*—sages who meditated in the forests and on the mountains. That tradition of reaching God through bhakti (devotion) endures with the sadhus. They are modern-day holy men who renounce all worldly pleasures—homes, clothes, sex and good food—in pursuit of God. You see them in yellow or ochre robes, flaunting the colours of sacrifice. Their bodies are often smeared with ash, a symbol of death, to show that they are in this world, but not of it. They carry nothing but a staff for support, a bowl for begging and sometimes a trident, the sign of Shiva. The sadhus are sages and wanderers, who walk the length of the country muttering hymns, never sleeping under a roof, never harming a creature. The more radical among them—Nanga sadhus—never wear a stitch. The sadhu's discipline is entirely self-imposed. But in India he never starves because the farsighted *rishis* had decreed: "The day a holy man does not get enough food, the end of the world is nigh."

For some sadhus, worship and devotion do not suffice. They punish themselves to wash away their imagined sins and temptations. Left: For these holy men in Hampi, white is a symbol of purity. It also means that they have castrated themselves, literally casting away sinful temptations. Above: A sadhu squatting beside a temple with the sum total of his wordly belongings. Temples are the roofs these sadhus are allowed to be under. Facing page: This holy man takes a serene gaze at life.

Islam: Among the Believers

India's Muslims might baffle their co-religionists elsewhere. On the one hand the community is scrupulously devout and numerically powerful— 120 million strong and growing. On the other hand it is also peculiarly Indian. It does not deny its past, which was moored in the caste system. Thus, you have the Rabari Muslims of Rajasthan, the finest cattle-breeders in India, who still shun beef. You see Muslim brides wear vermilion, the Hindu symbol of good marriage. And you have Muslims descended from Rajputs, the warrior caste, who still follow martial traditions and feel an affinity for Hindu Rajputs. They say: "We are divided by religion but united by blood." All this does not make them any less Muslim. They observe every practice and precept advocated by their religion. And five times a day, when the call to prayer hangs in the air, they turn towards Mecca and reaffirm their faith.

With their trimmed beards and their covered heads (left), Muslims are instantly recognisable in many parts of India. About one-eighth of Indians are Muslim. Below: Muslims turn to face Mecca and Allah is not forgotten even at a spot known for worldly magnificence—the compound of the Taj.

Living Saint

She is India's best-known and best-loved Christian. And people from every religion are welcomed to partake of the warmth of Mother Teresa's love for mankind. She expresses it in the most beautiful and poignant way conceivable, by making life and death a little easier for the poor around her. Every day, dozens of nuns from her "Missionaries of Charity" scour the streets to look for the homeless and the dying. Mother Teresa and her volunteers then bathe, feed and treat these unfortunate people. And if death is around the corner, they make sure it is not lonely. Today, the Roman Catholic nun who came to India from Albania to teach Geography runs more than 500 poor homes in 105 countries.

FESTIVALS OF INDIA

In India, the calendar on the wall does not consist of monotonous rows of dates marked in black. Every week or two there are splashes of red—public holidays—marking the coming of one festival or another. Till some years back, these festivals were invested with deep religious significance as different communities celebrated what was most important to them.

The farming class wallowed in Holi, an earthy festival of colours which roughly coincides with the onset of spring. Kings reaffirmed their patronage for the priestly classes on Rakshabandhan, the festival of protection. The warriors polished their weapons and made blood sacrifices on Vijayadashmi, the festival of victory. And on Deepawali, the festival of lights, the merchant class prayed to the goddess of prosperity and opened account books for the new year.

Interspersed with these were scores of other festivals, some local, some secular and some, like Christmas and Eid, international. Now all these festivals have become just celebrations of life in which everyone, irrespective of caste, community and religion, joins in and has fun. Most people who celebrate Christmas are Hindus. On Holi, most people who embrace each other are strangers. And on Durga Pooja, the festival of the most powerful Hindu goddess, those who fashion the idols are Muslims.

Ladakh, once an important trading post along the silk route, is now known as the land of Buddhist lamas. Almost every family contributes one son to monkhood. Above: Monks with their horns at the Gompa (temple) festival. Right: Festivals depict the clash between good and evil—the devil is startlingly masked. Below: A giant tanka (cloth painting) of the Buddha.

The monsoon has withdrawn, the crop is ready for harvest and Pongal, Tamil Nadu's festival of joy comes bursting forth. Bonfires are lit to chase evil away.
Top left: A woman traces a kilar (decorative design) with moistened rice flour. Top right and above: As blooms flourish in this season, their petals are used to decorate the floor and thank god.
Left: Women carry baskets on their heads. On Pongal day, the rice of the new harvest is cooked until it boils over. That is when the celebrations begin.

*T*richurpooram (left and facing page) is one of Kerala's most extravagant festivals. Set up as a friendly contest between two opposing teams who try to impress god, it includes a face-off involving 30 elephants that show off their decorative parasols, march to drum beats and try to overawe each other with sheer size. After midnight the elephants take a break and contestants light up the sky with blazing pyrotechnics, each more spectacular than the other.

*L*egend has it that an immensely powerful demon, who could not be defeated by any male, started conquering the Universe. So all the gods in heaven decide to pool their powers and create the ultimate form of Energy (Shakti). Lightning flashed, thunder boomed and Goddess Durga, an embodiment of female power, was born as the saviour of the Universe.
Above: Every year, devotees go in a procession with images of Durga astride her lion vanquishing the demons.
Right: Durga is also a symbol of fertility and hopeful mothers pray at her temple in Benares.

In predominantly Catholic Goa, a Hindu festival celebrating Goddess Durga lends a quaint charm. With baskets of flowers on their heads, devotees give it a Goan touch. Left: Celebrating the triumph of good over evil. Right: Young boys, with sacred threads on their bare bodies, affirm their bonds with God.

An evil demon swallowed the Sun God (Surya) and darkness descended on earth. It was only when the demon was slain that sunlight returned. That is how many Hindus perceive a solar eclipse. Right: In Kurukshetra, devotees gather before a solar eclipse to watch the Sun God battle the battle. Below: Some crouch, face down, as the tension grows. Bottom: A sadhu burrows his head in the sand to lend his support to the battling sun.

Deepawali

A filial son, a daring warrior, a loving husband with an ascetic's detachment, Rama was the ideal man. He gave up his kingdom and went into exile for 14 years, to honour a vow his father had made. There, a ten-headed demon kidnapped Rama's wife Sita. Aided by a monkey army, strengthened by the righteousness of his cause, Rama vanquished the demon in combat and returned home to reclaim his kingdom. The overjoyed populace lit up the streets with rows upon rows of lamps. The tradition endures. Deepawali (literally "rows of lamps") comes just as the first winter chills are in the air and the nights dark. But the lamps and the blazing fireworks of celebration chase the shadows away.

Holi

This festival is as earthy, as rugged and as physical as the farmers of North India who first popularised it. And, like most other Indian festivals, it is rooted in a myth. According to the story, Prahlad was a child devoted to the worship of the Lord. A demoness with a fireproof shawl jumped with him into a burning pyre. Her fireproof shawl could not however save her. On the other hand, the Lord made sure that Prahlad was unscathed. Throughout India, that has now become an excuse to celebrate. They soak each other in vegetable dye, they dunk each other in slush and water and they aim water-filled balloons at every passerby. And then they embrace. There is no malice in this horseplay. But water cannot immediately wash the dye away and remains of it linger on the face of even managers and bank presidents for weeks after the festival has passed.

Many Indian villages are conservative and frown upon boys and girls mingling freely with each other. But all barriers come crashing down around Holi time when womenfolk get drenched in colour. But they give as good as they get. Above: Strange hues light up the faces of these women.

SLICE OF LIFE

Everything in India seems high key. The colours are stark, the sounds are shrill, the smells are deep and penetrating and movement is sudden and expansive. It is almost as if everyone in a crowd of 900 million feels the need to stand up and be noticed. So the place is given to grand gestures and excessive expression. In the bazaars they don't merely peddle their wares. They tug at your sleeves, call to you, attract you with songs and dramatically

slash their prices for you. On the road you get the feeling that everyone is in a hurry and no one is getting anywhere. Drivers honk and curse as they find their paths blocked by lumbering bullock carts, serenely stopping time and traffic. Rip-off rap vies with ancient temple song festivals for attention while avant garde plays in English try to displace a dance-drama about the life of Lord Rama from the pop charts. It is all jostle and bustle. Everything leaps up at the same time to catch your eye. There is room for everyone but they would rather be a little more prominent.

Festivals are not a time for long faces. Above: A grim policeman controls crowds during a Goa festival while the mask behind him grins happily.

Have wheels, will travel. Above: A typical Indian street scene. Everyone is bumping into each other as rickshaws, pedestrians and vans try to squeeze onto a narrow road. Left: In Bombay, there is a method to the traffic madness. Right: When distances are long and vehicles are few and far between, everyone clambers atop overburdened vans like this one.

Indian Bazaar

The bazaar is more than a marketplace. It is a world by itself. In most parts of India, it doesn't just stretch along the road, it takes it over. The street becomes a courtyard on which hawkers squat and buyers wander from stall to stall. The air is filled with the cries of shopkeepers chanting their prices like a mantra, cajoling buyers, haggling with them. Nothing dims their energy—not the sweltering heat, not the scorn of passersby. The pungent smell of freshly ground spices is everywhere. The wares lie in incongruous heaps—watermelons, radio sets, shirts from Taiwan and handicrafts from the villages. And it is not just the goods that vie for your attention.

Sitting serenely under the shade of a tree at the edge of the bazaar, you might run into a barber gently trading gossip as he gives you a shave. Or a tailor who offers to stitch you a shirt while you suck at some ice-candy. You never quite know what the next stall might bring.

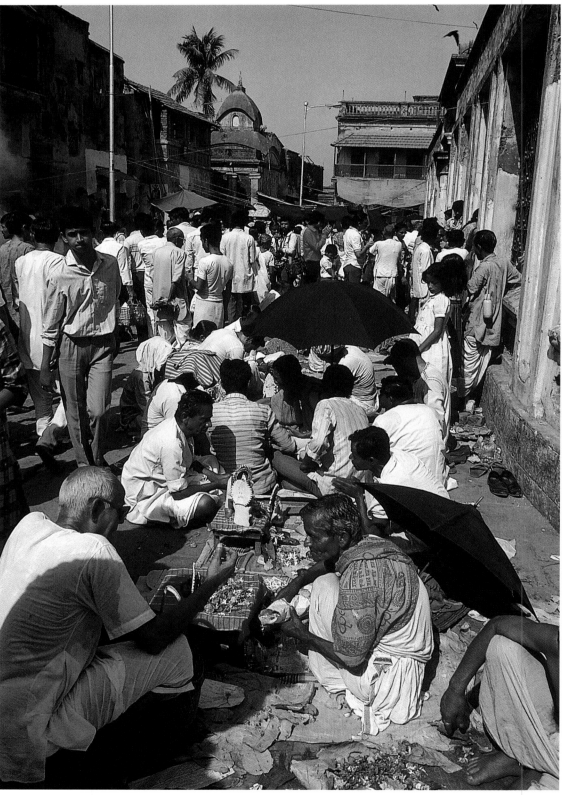

Preceding pages: An entire stretch of road in Goa is commandeered by fruit and vegetable sellers. Prices drop sharply around evening time as hawkers, with no storage facilities, try to dispose of goods that will not endure. Above: Indian hawkers are master salesmen, tempting passersby with auspicious colours at a Rangoli shop, glistening watered carrots and tantalisingly spread-out cosmetics. Right: The jostle for space and custom becomes more frantic as the new year festival approaches in Calcutta. Facing page: In Ernakulam, there is an entire market devoted just to fresh bananas.

The roadside bazaar has everything you can conceivably need. Facing page: A shirt for your back. Left: A quick bite of news. Above: An ice-cream man, whose roaming bicycle bell thrills children. Above left: Even someone to clean your ears.

Wedding of the Century

Lavish as Indian weddings are known to be, none has ever matched the extravagance of a recent one between the godson of a state chief minister and the granddaughter of an actor. More than 300,000 guests were invited for the wedding that took place in Madras. Two hundred truckloads of flowers carpeted an eight-kilometre road for the bridegroom, who rode a sandalwood carriage drawn by six Arabian horses. About 3,500 cooks worked round-the-clock to prepare 50 dishes for the guests. The wedding marquee spread across 12 hectares and the whole city of Madras was lighted up. Later the chief minister said that the US$35 million affair was ""just an ordinary wedding".

An Indian Wedding

It is like a soap opera, long, dramatic and full of special effects. The bride and the groom are no more than characters reading from a script someone else has written for them. They do not call the shots. They do not even choose each other. Most Indian weddings are "arranged" by parents and approved by astrologers. From this point, the similarities with theatre thickens. A vast audience is roped in, involving whole families, entire comunities and even the full complement of gods in the Hindu pantheon. A guest list of about 2,000 is more or less standard. The bride's make-up can take days as she is bathed in oils and unguents, decked out in outrageously expensive silk and jewellery and her palms are covered with intricate designs in henna. The groom comes on a horse, harking back to an ancient tradition in which he bore away the bride. Before him dance his relatives and friends, clogging the road and often letting off fireworks and even gunshots. The procession makes its way to the bride's house, which is swathed in hundreds of glittering strands of light. There, amid the chant of mantras that may take hours, the bride and groom take their vows before the Fire God. Often, this is the first glimpse the bride gets of the man she is to spend her life with. The bride's entire clan bursts into tears as she leaves her home, borne away in a palanquin. This, too, is part of custom.

Passing the Time

Killing time is an art in India and movies are the main instrument. Every Friday, when new films are released in halls all over the country, scores of tractors and bullock carts laden with families set out from the villages for a day out in town. Giant cinema hoardings dominate the skyline. So great is the demand that the Indian film industry churns out an average of 18 to 20 movies a week—the highest in the world—and a surprisingly large number of them are successful. Movie stars are revered. Many of them have been elected state chief ministers without a day's experience in politics. Another Western craze is cricket, played Indian style in every street and park, with bricks and shoes doubling as stumps. Crowds exceeding 100,000 queue up to watch international matches. But when it is too hot to play cricket and all the movie tickets have been sold out, Indians return to their ancient obsessions—kite-flying and mud-wrestling.

Time stands still for this couple in love (left). Above: Time explodes in fantastic hues for movie-goers. Right: Time is a whirl of a top. Below: Time tiptoes past these attentive readers.

The steam engine may be obsolete in most parts of the world but it continues to chug in certain parts of India. India also boasts of two of the oldest locomotives in the world (1873 vintage) which still huff and puff through the plains of Uttar Pradesh. One ancient steam engine even manages to pant up to Darjeeling.

Palace on Wheels

When the maharajahs travelled, they could not take their palaces with them. So they did the next best thing. They cocooned themselves in special train coaches that incorporated all the comfort and opulence of their living rooms. The Indian government has now acquired 13 such vintage carriages and strung them together to form the most extravagant train in Asia. It chugs on a steam engine across 2,500 kilometres of maharajah territory, stopping near forts and palaces and other remains of days gone by. Passengers are taken to these sights on caparisoned elephants and slouching camels. Back in the cool, dark comfort of their coaches, uniformed attendants wait on these maharajahs-for-a-week.

PART FOUR

ART AND ARCHITECTURE

Several millennia before critics, collectors and auction houses created an art market, there were the craftsmen of Indus Valley. Using primitive tools and outrageous imagination they fashioned magnificent figurines like the Dancing Girl, with her jaunty posture and impish smile, some 2,500 years before the birth of Christ.

This early artistic promise was to flower into a full-fledged tradition once religion came into the picture. India is perhaps the only country in the world where the arts and crafts are linked so closely to the gods that they have their own deity. This is the legend of Vishwakarma—Supreme Craftsman to the Gods, Lord of Many Arts, Father of Colour and Texture, Carpenter to the Gods, Designer of All Ornaments and Liberator of Imagination.

The legend was born during Vedic times, when the pantheon of Hindu gods was evolving and the need to express devotion was being felt. Shrines were not seen merely as structures in which people gathered to worship, but as real abodes of gods. Images in temples were not just abstract representations of deities. Instead, they were considered founts of true power. So the craftsmen worked as if something holy and mighty was taking shape in their hands.

Add to this the wealth of a kingdom and an increasing perfection of the craft and you will see why the temples and sculptures created around the 4th century A.D., known as the Golden Age of Indian art, are such masterpieces. The images are serene and lifelike. They are profusely decorated, marvellously sculpted and invested with such detail and zest that they seem to come alive.

All this while Buddhist kings too were erecting beautiful stupas, memorials which had a bewildering variety of images carved on them. The motto seemed to be: "Only the ornamental is beautiful".

But the years that followed the Golden Age were years of war and strife. From building beautiful temples, the kings started concentrating on mammoth forts, made for sturdiness rather than beauty, to weather the assaults of the invaders.

The next great architectural leap, ironically, was to start with a volley of mindless destruction. From the 8th century B.C. waves upon waves of invaders came from Central Asia and started pillaging ancient temples, sometimes razing them to the ground. In their place they started creating new monuments, supposedly Islamic in design. What they achieved instead was a fusion of two classical styles of architecture—Islamic and Hindu—and a typically Indian genre was born. This style reached its zenith in the most sublime of all monuments, the Taj Mahal.

Meanwhile, other forms of art have continued to thrive. Down the ages, ancient dance forms have been preserved in temples and palaces. They are still alive and throbbing with vitality today. The reign of the great Mughals saw some masterly miniature paintings come alive on canvas. And the British rule added the only arrow missing in the architectural quiver—a touch of Europe. Yes, the tradition of Vishwakarma continues to find a million delectable expressions.

The Sanchi stupa (left) is a magnificent dome-shaped Buddhist monument built more than 2,000 years ago by Emperor Ashoka. Above: The carved gateways (toranas) of the stupa are alive with Buddhist legends and symbols.

PRAYERS IN STONE

India's shrines are grand and complex affairs, as intricate as the religions that inspired them. It is obvious that the ancient architects who designed them thought they were really building homes where their gods would live. First came little jungle shrines whose very timbers were said to contain divine spirits. Then, in the third century B.C., Buddhist monks started hollowing out mountainsides, believing, for some reason, that the Buddha should stay in the bowels of the earth. They burrowed caves and created elaborately carved pillars, delicate paintings and lovingly sculpted statues. The Hindu shrine came into its own only in the 5th century A.D. when thousands of temples were built to honour different deities. In the eastern city of Bhubaneshwar alone, 700 temples were erected around a sacred lake. The temple started evolving from simple, two-room structures to bigger, more complex, multi-chambered ones. It developed spires that were supposed to reach out to the heavens and attract the gods. Its walls became the canvas for intricate sculptures, showing nymphs and midgets, kings, dancing girls and monsters. And just when it seemed temples could get no grander, Muslim invaders brought a touch of Persia to the dry plains of India. The huge domes and arched recesses of the mosques they built now beckon believers from all parts of the world.

About 800 years ago, devotees in a small Orissa town decided to build a magnificent horse-drawn chariot for the Sun God. For 16 years, 1,200 artisans laboured on the Konarak Sun Temple, engraving the wheels of the chariot, giving detail to seven magnificent steeds until it seemed that the sun would really start its journey from here. Though the central tower of the temple collapsed, the remains are still fascinating.
Facing page: Women pay homage to the Sun God in Konarak. They see it as the giver of all life. Above: An erotic detail carved on the temple. Above right: Detail from the Parasurameshwar Temple. This temple is even older than the one in Konarak. It was built in the 7th century.

Among the stone sermons of Bhubaneshwar, the Mukteshwara Temple (above) stands out. It has an ornamental interior, a sculptured gateway and walls lush with intricate nymphs and serene gods.
Far left: Figures of Jain saints at a temple.
Left: Amidst the rocks in Badami, a splendid mosque rises.
Overleaf: A 6th century cave sculpture in Badami adds a purely aesthetic dimension to this city of gods.

Ajanta and Ellora

During the second century B.C., a bunch of Buddhist monks went looking for the perfect place to celebrate their faith. They found a mountainside with blue skies above and a river wending its way below. Into this mountainside they carved some of the most beautiful cave temples known to man. In all, they excavated 29 caves. The walls are decorated with sensational murals, painted ostensibly to educate the monks about the temptations Buddha had to give up to attain salvation. There are scenes from palace life. They show caparisoned elephants, buxom maidens, pearl necklaces and tiaras of gold crowns. Other frescoes illustrate popular folktales of the day. Then there are stupas embellished with carvings of the Buddha. Around these marched processions of monks, chanting scriptures and hoping to achieve salvation.

Ellora is unique in the sense that its 34 rock-cut temples represent not one but three different faiths—Buddhism, Jainism and Hinduism. All these structures were scooped out of sheer rock a thousand years ago. Above: Kailash Temple in Ellora.

Khajuraho

In 900 A.D., a minor prince from the Chandella Rajput clan decided to make his capital, Khajuraho, a home for the gods. Over the next 150 years, 22 temples were erected, each depicting a wonderful, extraordinary notion that was taking root in Hinduism around that time. The walls of the temples were carved with figures of voluptuous maidens making love to handsome princes in a bewildering variety of poses. This sexual union between man and woman was supposed to show the union between the human and the divine. Also, far from being frowned upon, sex was supposed to be part of the "flow of life" and ultimately related to god.

Even today, an erotic dance festival takes place every year to keep the notion alive. The dome spires of the temples rise upwards, like foothills towards the Himalayas. This is supposed to show that every step raises us toward god.

An erotic panel in a Khajuraho temple (facing page). While Khajuraho is now known primarily for these sensuous depictions, they form only a small part of the temples' architecture. The main purpose is to lead the eye from earth to heaven, combining worldly pleasures with spiritual bliss. This fusion comes out in the sculptures at Khajuraho (left) as well as the Vishwanath Temple in Khajuraho (above).

Temple-Cities of the South

In North India, the temples rose vertically towards the sky. In South India, they spread along the ground, growing in every direction, until they became cities by themselves. As the temples grew more popular, concentric rings of walls were added around the original sanctuaries, more shrines were raised and dormitories were constructed for pilgrims. Merchants who came to cater to the pilgrims set up permanent stalls within the precincts. The Arunacaleshwara Temple in Tamil Nadu is one such temple-city.

The sheer expanse of south Indian holy cities is startling. Left: Temples in Badami, Karnataka, stretch to the horizon. Above: Monolithic temples in Tamil Nadu.

A Touch of Islam

As soon as Muslim kings had conquered a land, it was customary for them to build a mosque there, partly as a token of their gratitude to Allah and partly because Islam prefers congregational prayers. In India, one of the first mosques was built on the ruins of 27 temples that were destroyed to make way for it. At first, these mosques were hotchpotch affairs—remains of the original, short temple pillars were placed one above another to build the lofty minarets of the mosque. But gradually, mosque architecture became an art form by itself, as Hindu artisans learned to etch lofty domes, sleek minarets, floral motifs and even quotations from the Quran.

Sikh Temple

Some 400 years ago, Guru Arjun, a leader of the Sikh faith, raised a small temple in the midst of a placid pool. Inside this structure he placed the *Guru Granth Sahib*, the holy book of the Sikhs. Since then the temple at Amritsar has been the holiest of Sikh shrines. In the 19th century, the temple was rebuilt in marble and its domes covered with 400 kilograms of gold leaf. Since then, it has been called the Golden Temple.

The Sikh religion, which was given shape in the 15th century by Guru Nanak, shuns idol worship. It reveres only its holy book, the Granth Sahib, which is kept in the Golden Temple (left). Above left: The Moti Masjid (Pearl Mosque) in Agra got its name from a huge pearl that once dangled from its ceiling. Facing page: A young Brahmin boy at a temple in Chidambaram.

LAND OF THE MAHARAJAHS

While India's shrines have endured the ravages of time, many of its once mighty forts and palaces are in ruins. Splendid as they might have been, their glory lasted only as long as the dynasties that created them. New rulers built new structures while the old ones withered through disrepair. There was no one to maintain them, unlike the temples that were kept intact by pilgrims and devotees. So, of the commanding ramparts that drew their magic circles around ancient kings there are now only memories and the odd painting in some rock cave.

But there is no doubt that the kings did themselves well. In the Vijayanagara Empire, which a scholar from Europe has described "as large as Rome", the king's palace enclosed "a space greater than all the castles of Lisbon". The splendour comes through even in the sorry skeleton that survives. And there is no doubt they were indulgent. A mighty palace, shaped like a ship, still stands at Mandu.

The best preserved forts and palaces of medieval times are in the Rajput belt of Madhya Pradesh and Rajasthan (literally "Land of Kings"). The Rajputs, said to have descended from the Scythians, ended up as defenders of Hinduism against Muslim invaders. From the outside, their forts are sprawling instruments of war, generally perched atop hills several hundred metres high, surrounded by rugged walls and lofty gateways designed to withstand battle rams. But inside are a series of delicate buildings with profuse carvings and gardens where princes rested.

Purely decorative palace architecture came into its own only around the 18th century. Palaces of those days have exquisite paintings and latticed windows that were clearly not designed to keep invaders at bay. Many of these palaces have now been converted into luxury hotels and are paying for themselves for the first time in their history.

Rajput rulers combined military valour with a taste for good living. Above: This palace in Jodhpur has a magnificent gilded ceiling inside a fort that was designed to keep invaders at bay. Right: Work on the formidable Gwalior Fort started in the 6th century and culminated in the 15th century when Raja Mansingh put the final touches on one of the most remarkable citadels in India. Facing page: Hawa Mahal, the Palace of the Winds, in Jaipur. Women used to sit modestly behind its 953 ornate windows and watch the world go by.

Princely states have been abolished but former rulers are still treated like kings in many parts of India. Above: Maharajah Bibhut Narayan Singh on his marble bench. Overleaf: Rajput rulers built Jodhpur as a "Blue City".

The Jodhpur Fort (below) is more than 120 metres high, sits on a rugged hill and can only be reached after crossing seven gateways. More recently in 1942, a Jodhpur ruler had a 347-room palace built for himself, making it one of the largest private residences in the world. Right and far right: Signs of times gone by. Itmad-ud-Daulah, a Mughal prime minister's tomb in Agra which some call as beautiful as the Taj, and the ruins of the Golconda Fort in Hyderabad.

When Prince Albert, consort of Queen Victoria, visited Jaipur in 1883, its rulers ordered the entire city painted pink as a gesture of welcome. Since then, the label and the colour has stuck and Jaipur is still known as the Pink City.
Far left: The city palace, where Jaipur's erstwhile ruling family lives, also houses an intriguing museum. Among other things there are two large urns that carried a six-month supply of Ganges water for a Rajput ruler who visited London. Left: The upkeep of the royal residence is expensive and to defray costs, a Jaipur palace is now a hotel.

Mark of Death

The massive walls of Rajasthan's forts were often powerless against the swift and tactically superior marauders from Central Asia. When defeat was inevitable, these forts became the stage for one of the most poignant traditions of the Rajputs. The warriors would don saffron, the colour of sacrifice, throw open the gates of the fort and ride out to meet their death on the battlefield. Their wives would then gather solemnly before a vast pyre, say their last prayers and, one by one, immolate themselves. The custom was called *Jauhar* and many of Rajasthan's imposing forts have seen such immolations in their compounds. In Chittorgarh Fort alone, Rajput women have met this fiery end on three separate occasions. The same is true of the 85-year-old Jaisalmer Fort. And at the entrance of Meherangrah Fort in Jodhpur, you can still see stone hand-prints of women who hurled themselves into the pyre rather than be captured alive by invaders.

Indians have romanced death, often making it heroic. Left: A Sikh warrior who pledges death before dishonour.
Above: The painted feet symbolise sati— a Rajput custom in which widows hurled themselves into their husband's pyre.

Fatehpur Sikri

The fort at Fatehpur Sikri was an act of faith and gratitude by the great Mughal emperor, Akbar. At the peak of his power, despite having hundreds of wives, Akbar did not have a son to succeed him to the throne. So he visited Salim Chishti, a holy man who stayed in the village of Sikri. The hermit blessed Akbar and in no time the rejuvenated king had three sons from three different wives. Since the holy man would not move to Agra, Akbar decided to move his entire capital to Sikri in his honour. He built a wonderful complex of palaces and battlements in red sandstone. To commemorate his military conquests, he erected a 50-metre high gateway called Buland Darwaza. But this perfect palace city also had its lighter side. A piece of ground was set aside as a real life chessboard on which the pieces were pretty slaves. The emperor would direct the game from his five-storey high Panch Mahal and apparently whoever won could take the girls home. But after a mere 15 years, Akbar had to abandon this city in pristine condition because there wasn't enough water.

Salim Chishti told Emperor Akbar that he would have a son, and the emperor named the son Salim after the holy man. Legend has it that Salim Chishti told Akbar he would die the day the young prince recited something from memory. Sure enough, the day three-year-old Salim recited a couplet, the saint took ill and breathed his last. In his memory, Akbar built a magnificent tomb at Fatehpur Sikri (above).

DELHI—WALKING WITH HISTORY

It is a city with memories that stretch back two millennia and a history that spills out of its walls and pavements. It is also a sprawling metropolis with eight million people to house and not much time to dwell on the past. Never mind the fact that the city has been built and destroyed seven times as successive waves of rulers decided it was an ideal capital and tried to mould it in their own image. Never mind that other cities treat relics from their past with a hushed reverence. Delhi, today, has become a kind of museum which children dirty and where people live as if it were the most natural thing in the world. They have found new uses for its ancient monuments. Archaeological milestones are now just names of bus stops. Tughlaqabad, a 14th-century capital of a dominant dynasty, is now a firing range. Purana Quila, an emperor's fort in the 16th century (which itself was built over third century ruins), now forms the boundary to the Delhi Zoo. Even New Delhi, the graceful city of wide roads and sprawling gardens planned by British architect Lutyens, is no more and no less than an office block to tens of thousands of civil servants. But something of a sense of history survives in the poetry festivals that recall the days of Mughal grandeur and in trips to ancient shrines where people mutter the same prayers their ancestors did, a thousand years back.

Delhi is decorated with the tombs of those who built the city. Right: When Mughal emperor Humayun died in the 16th century, his widow Haji Begun built him a tomb with arched entrances, resplendent domes and sprawling gardens. This is said to have inspired a better-known mausoleum, the Taj. Humayun's wife is also buried in the same complex. Above: One of the last surviving examples of Mughal architecture is the tomb of Safdarjung, built in 1754. Facing page, top left and right: The tomb of Tughlaq dynasty ruler Ghiyas-ud-Din and the Lodhi tombs are set in lush gardens that have become popular picnic spots.

A 16th century mosque (below) still stands amidst the ruins of Delhi's Old Fort. Bottom: Raja Jai Singh II, a Rajput ruler fascinated by astronomy, built a series of quaintly shaped structures to help him with his celestial calculations. Vast sun dials, erected in 1724, still attract curious visitors.

Mughal Memories

A solitary soldier blows his bugle to announce that dawn has come to Red Fort with military precision. A regiment stirs and the fort rouses as it has for the past 400 years. But so much has changed. Where Shah Jahan once sat on his peacock throne of emerald and gold, there now paces an impatient army officer eyeing the clock. The gardens where princesses lounged are now crammed with car parks, jugglers and hawkers selling balloons. The handsome boulevard where a canal glistened so brightly at night that people called it Chandni Chowk ("Moonlit Plaza") is now a screaming, rushing, kicking, haggling bunch of humanity, bumping from shop to shop. Every step that follows is alive with history and irony. Sweetmeats are sold at the spot where Persian invader Nadir Shah had 30,000 people slaughtered on a single Sunday afternoon. The house of India's greatest romantic poet, Ghalib, is now a coal-shed. Yes, time has passed but history keeps returning to old Delhi. Long after the passing of the Mughals, India claimed its independence from the British at the exact spot from which Shah Jahan had ruled.

Symbols of power from different eras stand proud in Delhi.
Above: The Red Fort, from which the Mughals ruled. Left: Rashtrapati Bhawan, where India's head of state, now stays.

The russet sandstone walls of the Red Fort (above) still show glimpses of forgotten glory. The delicate white marble Pearl Mosque, where emperors spoke to god, is still intact. So, too, is an inscribed couplet that says: "If there is a Paradise on Earth, It is This, It is This". But Shah Jahan's peacock throne has been carted away by invaders.
Left: A rickshaw puller awaits tourists outside the fort.

*O*ld Delhi is one of the most densely-populated areas in the world. Above: Matchbox houses dot the skyline. Below: The bustle of Chandni Chowk.

Remains of the Raj

The eighth city of Delhi, built from scratch by the British in the 1930s, was intended to be a piece of Europe transplanted on Indian soil. The roads are wide and tree-lined. The mansions of ministers stand withdrawn, with immense green lawns and tall silent gates. The houses of Parliament have elegant curves and uncomplicated lines. Somehow, the air of breathtaking spaciousness and solemn dignity that New Delhi exudes seems unreal in a chatty, bubbly, earthy place like India. But all that is set right on January 26, Republic Day, when camels, floats, people in bright red turbans and all the colours of India descend on New Delhi for the largest parade in the world.

*T*he 42-metre high India Gate (top left) is inscribed with names of 13,516 British and Indian soldiers who died fighting near Afghanistan in World War I. It was built in 1931. A more recent addition is Amar Jyoti, the Eternal Flame, that burns here in the memory of the Unknown Soldier killed in the war with Pakistan in 1971.

TAJ MAHAL

Its beauty is almost a cliche. Pictures of its domes and towers have passed before your eyes so often that you tell yourself it will not surprise you. That it is, somehow, overrated. But go there and you feel you are in the presence of magic, of god, of the pain of a love irredeemably lost and of perfection that happens just once in a lifetime, almost by chance. It is almost a spiritual experience. You feel humbled and realise that it is impossible to arrest the beauty of the Taj Mahal in a picture frame. Either the photographer has to step back to capture the superb balance of its proportions, the stretch of its minarets and the rounding of its dome. Or, more rarely, he zooms in to record the almost-feminine carvings on its walls and the mournful silence of its crypts. Neither of this quite matches the unfolding wonder that grips you—from the breathless sight of its white marble glistening in the pool to the startled examination of its exquisitely inlaid stones.

And then there is its history. Emperor Shah Jahan was so completely enamoured of his wife, that as she lay dying he promised to construct the world's most magnificent mausoleum in her memory. White marble was carted from mines in Rajasthan. Artisans were hired from every corner of the country. Hindu architects worked hand in hand with advisors from Persia while the emperor himself oversaw the entire operation. Twenty thousand men slaved for 22 years to create what the poet Rabindranath Tagore has called "a teardrop on the cheek of time". And then, legend says that Shah Jahan had their hands chopped off so that these master builders could never construct anything as beautiful. Well, Taj Mahal cannot be replicated. And perhaps Shah Jahan, later imprisoned by his son Aurangzeb, had ample time to reflect on that as he spent his last days gazing at his legacy from a fort across the Taj. He was buried in a crypt next to Mumtaz Mahal, his beloved wife.

WESTERN INFLUENCES

It is impossible for a people to live almost 200 years in a foreign land and not leave an imprint on its buildings and monuments. So, too, with the British. Of course, climate did not permit them to replicate British housing in India's dusty hamlets. But buildings that served as the nerve centres of government all over India—and are still in active use—were clearly Victorian in conception. The influence is even more obvious in Chandigarh and New Delhi—two cities specially erected by the British to bring Europe to India. And the wide,

white structures in army cantonments, with high ceilings, broad columns and manicured lawns, could be standing in any English countryside. But it is not the Britishers alone who left their mark. The Portuguese who came to Goa in 1510 and stayed on until the 20th century built exuberant, baroque-style churches and painted their villas green to add a dash of Lisbon to Goa. In Pondicherry, where the French ruled for centuries, policemen wear French-style caps while statues of Joan of Arc and Governor-General Dupleix soar in the city.

Right: Resembling a sleepy French provincial town, Pondicherry looks markedly different from the rest of South India. Splendid old buildings, such as this one, are some of the many legacies the French left behind.

Victoria Memorial in Calcutta (above) is an enduring testimony to the Raj in more ways than one. Not only is the architecture British, but the building also houses Victorian memorabilia including old letters and documents. Right: This room, with its Victorian furniture and British portraits, could easily be part of a London manor. In fact it is in New Delhi. Facing page: With their carved pillars, overhanging balconies and stained glass, many Goan houses retain strong Portuguese influences.

DANCE—ART IN MOTION

It was a tradition steeped in antiquity but it survived right up to this century. Indian temples, especially in the South, would recruit hundreds of pretty young women as Devadasis, servants of God. These women were trained to dance before the Lord, they never married and they spent their entire lives in the temple. Not everyone was eligible for the job. The qualifications laid down for a good dancer were: "The person should be handsome, sweet in speech, born of good family, sweet-voiced, quick-witted and confident." For these women, dance was a form of worship, one of the 16 offerings that the Lord accepts. That is how dance has traditionally been viewed in India and it is not surprising that it was born and flourished in the temples. Its purpose was to enchant the deity through *tandava* or rhythm and *lasya*, the use of gestures, poses and facial movement to express various shades of feeling. These basics still hold, and even though the Devadasi system has died out, it takes six to eight years of devoted training, before a dancer masters the intricacies of the art. Many dances are still religious in their orientation, like Kathakali with its fascinating masks and Manipuri, a sinuous celebration of Krishna. But the range of Indian dances has now broadened to include other influences as well such as Kathak, a dance that developed in the palaces. There are also vibrant harvest dances, such as Bhangra and Dandiya, which need no stage other than green fields rolling in the background.

Odissi, from the eastern state of Orissa, is perhaps India's most lyrical dance form. The dancers, such as the one above, borrow postures from the carvings at the Sun Temple in Konarak and infuse them with the ecstasy of devotion to Krishna. The entire culture of the region is depicted in those intricate movements. Right: Portrait of dancer from Mahabalipuram, Tamil Nadu.

Indian dance is passed on from generation to generation through the guru shishya parampara, the teacher-disciple tradition. Right: For the students at this dance school in Thanjavur, the gurus (teachers) are like parents, passing on their knowledge but expecting complete devotion in return. A student may learn formally for up to 10 years and keep going back for more. Above: Rajasthan folk artistes start young.

While classical dance and music (below) may have a rigid structure and rules, folk traditions fly free. They are a spontaneous outpouring of joy, not hemmed in by technique, as seen in Goa's folk dance (left) and the tribal dances of Orissa (right). While classical dance borrows its themes from religious texts, folk dance does so from local myths and legends.

Kathakali is a dance form requiring immense technique and endless stamina. A single performance can stretch up to eight hours. The actors depict characters in the Mahabharata—gods and demons, mortals and supernatural beings. All the dancers are male. They combine dance with dialogue and acting skills. Right: The dancers in huge skirts and headdresses wear elaborate make-up. Below: The Cochin Kathakali theatre parading its skills.

Kathakali

To the uninititated it may look weird, but to connoisseurs Kathakali is one of India's most fascinating dance forms. It is a kind of pantomime in which stories of Rama and Krishna are depicted through signs and gestures, with vigorous music in the background. The make-up of the actors borders on the bizarre as their faces are caked in garish colours. But this is deliberate. It is supposed to evoke an otherworldly atmosphere. The make-up takes at least four hours. The actor lies flat on his back while pastes of flour in different colours are applied on the face like some elaborate mask. Each colour is said to have its own significance. Experienced actors usually fall asleep while the make-up artiste is at work.

CRAFTS

Aurangzeb, the pious 17th century Mughal monarch, was once outraged to see his daughter Zebunissa make a public appearance in the nude. When he scolded her, she showed him that she was wearing a muslin drape, wrapped seven times around her body. Some master craftsman had laboured for years and woven it so fine that it seemed invisible to the naked eye. The story may be apocryphal but it sums up the creed of Indian craftsmen. Their patience is endless. Hours and years mean nothing to them as they pursue traditions as old as the country itself. Above all, Indian craft is based on painstaking effort. You still find doddering old weavers in Kashmir trying to fashion metre-long pashmina shawls that can pass through a signet ring. Masters of metalwork hunch over their creations chasing floral patterns on brass. The more humble potters of the villages may be less skilled, but they are equally devoted to their craft. Day after day they rise before dawn, squat around their humming wheel and massage wet clay into pitchers and pots. Saree-makers knot and dye every individual strand of silk as they weave fascinating designs into lengths of cloth. Many of these centuries-old skills had all but perished during the 19th century. A government board set up in 1952 has consciously been reviving them—partly to provide jobs to villagers and partly to preserve a heritage that no amount of money can buy.

Mughal rulers brought formal gardens, with petals and vines, to Kashmir. Kashmiri carpet weavers (above) have returned the compliment by weaving Mughal motifs into their creations.

For centuries, Rajasthani tribal women have been designing and fashioning their own flamboyant dresses. Now, a growing market has induced them to commercialise their embroidery and mirrorwork (right).
Above: A potter in Tamil Nadu conjuring up a vase while an artisan works on creating the Nataraja, which depicts Shiva as the master of dance.
Left: Rajasthan sarees, woven and dyed, stretch out like art forms.
Overleaf: A masterpiece takes birth.

MASTERS OF THE BRUSH

The opulence borders on the obscene. Merchants sip wine in cups of gold. Hefty slaves scurry to do their masters' bidding. Bold young women seduce impressionable princes. Lust and temptation are everywhere. Some ancient painter brought alive an entire world on the rocky canvas of Ajanta's cave walls as far back as the 2nd century B.C.

But after this magical flourish, the art of painting remained in limbo for a long time as the focus shifted to sculpting and architecture. It was only in the 16th century that three distinct genres developed. First came miniatures of courtly life, birds and flowers. Then evolved the Rajput style, which centred around the life and loves of Lord Krishna. Finally, portrait-painting came to India. One still find relics from those days like in impressions of scowling men in moustaches and embroidered turbans. Later, Mughal emperor Aurangzeb tried to stamp out painting altogether, claiming that it blasphemously imitated God's creativity. He ordered all paintings on his palace walls to be plastered over, but by now the flood was unstoppable.

Frescoes in Ajanta (right) were meant to depict the life and times of Buddha as well as the many legends of the day. They are surprisingly well-preserved more than 2,000 years later.
Above: Royal families started patronising portrait makers in the 16th century.

Women in India often get local artists to decorate their houses with "protective symbols". Below, right: A couple of tigers stand guard at this house. Below: A "Pattachitra" painter from Orissa illustrates folktales.

INDIA
THROUGH THE EYES OF PAINTERS

British painters were fascinated by the opulence and indulgences of the maharajahs. This 18th century lithograph depicts a favourite pastime of Indian princes—the elephant fight. Two bulls, hemmed in by big crowds, egged on by sticks and drums, attacked each other until one was fatally wounded.

*N*othing has changed in 300 years. This medieval painting shows women floating lamps along the Ganges as they celebrate Deepawali. The vegetation around the river may have vanished, but the custom still endures in Hardwar.

This 19th century lithograph shows an infant's funeral rites. Hindus believe that, unlike adults who get their karma (the fruit of their deeds), infants are untarnished. There is no need to cremate them and they pass directly into heaven through the Ganges.

With sandalwood paste across his forehead and his colourful headdress marking him out as a high-born, a South Indian Brahmin is serene at a kinsman's funeral. Brahmins never mourned death as they believed it meant salvation.

*B*ell in hand, a Brahmin couple walk along a Tamil Nadu street in this 19th century painting. Untouchables could not enter temples in those days and had to stand away from Brahmins, lest the high-borns be polluted by their shadows.

*A*n 1838 miniature shows the Mughal emperor Bahadurshah Zafar puffing on his tubed pipe.
This is one of the last known pieces of Mughal art, which declined after it was actively
discouraged by Emperor Aurangzeb, a religious fanatic.

*J*ahangir, one of the greatest patrons of art in India, is the man credited with importing European art techniques into India. This 17th century miniature depicts him receiving a learned treatise from one of the scholars at his court. Some miniatures depict him with a halo around his head.

The Thanjavur school of painting focuses on the various facets of Lord Krishna. This one shows the earthy deity flanked by two pretty maidens, obviously enjoying himself. Krishna shows that spiritual bliss is not divorced from physical joy.

Another offering from the Thanjavur school. This one depicts Krishna as a boisterous child. The central devotee of cowherds, he was known to have loved butter as a child. When his mother denied him this, he stole it with divine licence.

*T*hough Mughal painting declined in the 17th century, the techniques spread to Rajput kingdoms. The themes were indigenous. This miniature from Udaipur shows the Hindu Goddess Kali wearing a garland of demon heads. Her four hands bear weapons of destruction.

This contemporary lithograph is one of India's most popular paintings. It depicts Lord Shiva and his consort Parvati with their elephant-headed son Ganesha. Many million reproductions of this painting adorn Hindu homes, where it is worshipped.

This old Jain painting shows the founder of the faith, Mahavira, standing tall beneath a giant arch, dwarfing the rigid Brahminical codes, represented by two tiny figures.

*A*nother Jain watercolour. Jain paintings are among the very few works of Indian art known
to have been done between the 13th and 16th centuries. This one shows three holy figures
being honoured

*T*his Buddhist tanka (cloth painting) shows the courtly joys and pleasures that surrounded Prince Siddharta (later to become Buddha). At this stage of his life, he was unaware of suffering.

One day, Siddharta came face to face with the ugliness of the world. He realised that, away from his princely cocoon, there was death, disease, war, destruction and the suffering depicted in this tanka.

This painting shows the final phase of the Buddha's evolution. He attained Nirvana (salvation) when enlightenment came to him under the Bodhi tree in Gaya.

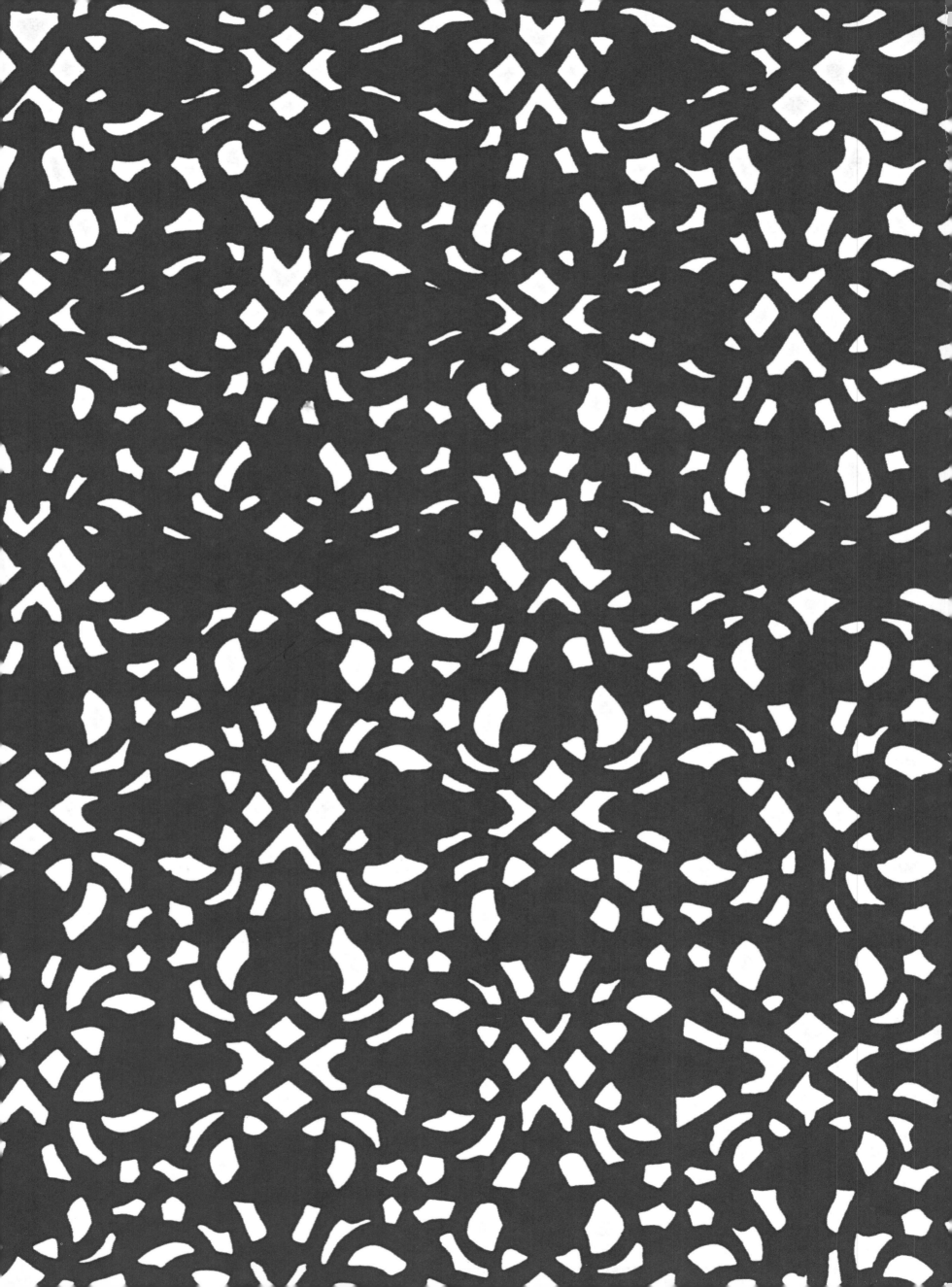